ICARUS

14

ROGER ROSEN
Editor

PATRA McS. SEVASTIADES
Commissioning Editor

K. MELISSA CERAR
Assistant Editor

LAURA C. REYBOLD
Editorial Assistant

BETTY BRINKERHOFF
Copy Editor

GINA STRAZZABOSCO
Editorial Consultant

JEFF DONALDSON-FORBES
Production Manager

KIM SONSKY
Production Consultant

JENNIFER CROFT
Publicity Manager

STEVEN K. SHAW
Financial Manager

AZAR BOUJARAN
Subscriptions

SELVIN MARROQUIN
Subscriptions Assistant

ISOBEL DIZENGOFF
ELIZABETH BURDIAN
Circulation

Cover by Chris Hyde

Icarus 14, Spring 1994
ISBN 0-8239-1810-6

ICARUS
NEW WRITING FROM AROUND THE WORLD

Icarus (ISSN 1054-1381) is published quarterly for $35.80 per year by The Rosen Publishing Group, Inc. Second class postage pending at New York, NY. POSTMASTER: Send address changes to: *Icarus*, 29 E. 21st Street, New York, NY 10010. Subscription correspondence should be addressed to: *Icarus*, 29 E.21st Street, New York, NY 10010.

Icarus welcomes submissions. Manuscripts must be accompanied by a stamped, self-addressed envelope. Editorial correspondence should be addressed to: The Editor, *Icarus*, 29 E. 21st Street, New York, NY 10010.

Contents

Introduction

The stories of women constitute more than half of human history. Owing to historical attitudes that downplayed or dismissed the significance of women's contributions, many of those histories have been buried along with the energetic women who lived them out: women who managed households in the absence of amenities we now take for granted—indoor plumbing, electricity, refrigeration, hot running water, washing machines, and prepared food; who took the major role in teaching their children the fundamentals of language, religion, social graces, and hygiene; artists, domestic workers, field hands, prostitutes, nuns. Many lived in obscurity or in exploitative circumstances owing to their gender, whereas fathers, brothers, husbands, and sons held a more elevated status on the social and legal ladder and thus greater latitude in their options. Forbidden to possess property, women and their children were more often societally consigned to the status of chattel.

What is a woman? Simone de Beauvoir filled two volumes in attempting to answer that for herself, considering everything from biology to literature to history. "One day I wanted to explain myself to myself," she writes, ". . . And it struck me with a sort of surprise that the first thing I had to say was 'I am a woman.'" Women have been defined, and often define themselves, by their relationships. Our language reflects this. The Anglo-Saxon word *wifman* from which springs our contemporary word "woman" was a combination of the words *wif*, a wife, and *man*, which in its original sense was a gender-neutral term meaning human being or person. Thus a woman is a wife-person, a person married to, or expected to marry, a man. But this and related expectations are the very ideas that have been put to the test most rigorously over the course of the twentieth century, and it is striking that many current crises at home and abroad are bound up in the question of women's true identity.

In a wrenching reassessment of an idea once widely viewed as inviolable, women have recently been ordained to the Anglican priesthood. U.S. Navy personnel of both sexes can now be assigned to duty on combat aircraft and ships. The ramifications of these seismic shifts are profound and sure to be felt—and resisted—for some time. American jurists and government officials grapple with the question of whether to deport or provide asylum to an illegal alien from Nigeria who seeks to protect her American-born daughters from the custom of genital mutilation. And in an attempt to highlight the way toys can encourage sexism and violence, a "guerrilla group," the Barbie Liberation Organization, transplanted Barbie's voice box into GI Joes in toy stores around the nation and placed warmongering GI Joe voice programs into Barbies. In this charged context, we set out to publish *Icarus* issue 14, "A Circle of Women: Stories of the Sisterhood."

We wrestled at length with this theme and in the end found it more compelling to leave to others the publication of invaluable materials about trends in feminism, antifeminism, and the feminist debate, and to prepare instead a collection focusing on the stories of women. One will find threads of the debate within these pieces and evidence to support a variety of positions. In the end, it is at the level of the individual life that the tension between society and person is played out.

We are delighted to open doors to women's experiences and often hard-won perspectives, from the tortured life of Natalie, alone on the street beside her shopping cart but befriended by a compassionate neighbor, to fashion-conscious Angelina on holiday in America with her parents, to the uncomprehending guilelessness of the child of a concentration camp survivor wandering through the world of her parents' war-scarred memory. And insofar as each selection explores the human condition, this issue is pertinent to readers of both sexes.

Women worldwide are still being paid less, receiving inferior education and medical care, and having less political voice than their male counterparts. In some cases, as in China, they are victims of infanticide simply because of their gender. This collective debasement of women is a ghastly consequence of ignorance. Issues surrounding gender are rarely simple. But it is important to work for the day when the birth of a child of either sex is met with equal joy. It is our hope that this international collection of writing will broaden the appreciation of women of all ages, races, and nationalities, each meriting fair treatment by dint of her humanity.

Patra McSharry Sevastiades
Commissioning Editor

Maxine Clair was born and raised in Kansas City, Kansas. She received a Bachelor of Science degree in medical technology from the University of Kansas and subsequently worked for fifteen years as a medical technologist. In 1982, she resigned as chief technologist at Children's Hospital National Medical Center in Washington, D.C., to pursue a Master of Fine Arts degree in creative writing. She received the degree from American University in 1984.

Ms. Clair, who has taught at American University, currently teaches writing at George Washington University. She has served on the board of the Washington Writers Publishing House and currently serves on the executive board of the Poetry Committee of Greater Washington. Her short stories have appeared in *Antietam Review* and *The Kenyon Review*.

Ms. Clair lives in a suburb of Washington. The following selection is an excerpt from her forthcoming book *Rattlebone*, which will be published by Farrar, Straus and Giroux in June.

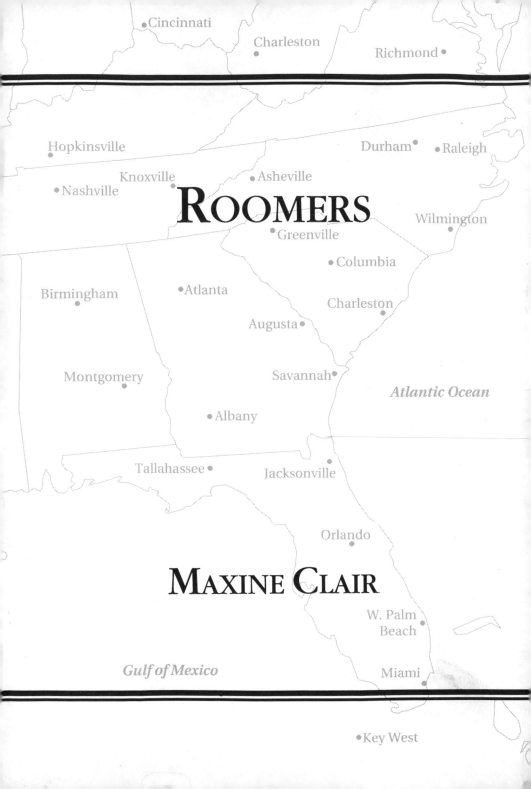

ROOMERS

MAXINE CLAIR

their undershirt and house shoes.

"Who're you?" Pemberton asked her. She told him who she was.

"I was told you might have a room to rent," she said.

"Depends," I said over Pemberton's shoulder. He would've stood there all day hemmin and hawin.

She'd done been down at the teachers' college two years and finished up at the university. They'd just hired her on up here in Rattlebone to teach the third grade at Stowe. She said her people were from down south somewhere, I done forgot where, but said she was raised in Ohio. Talked real proper. Pemberton liked proper talkers.

"We might have something," I said. "Come on, I'll show you the place." I sent Pemberton on back to his newspaper.

Long time ago, fact, soon as we got our first place, Pemberton wanted to take in roomers. No indeedy, I said. True, Pemberton was at the packing house then, working nights, but I didn't want nobody living with us right away.

Them wasn't no good times for us. We hadn't done been married a year when I up and got pregnant. Pemberton is the living proof that some men act a fool when their wife is carrying a child. I don't know if Pemberton just didn't know what to do with himself or what, but he started running around with a woman that lived a block over from us. Mamie Turner. High-yellow woman with the long hair and what I call a large following, you know, big hips. I never knew much about the woman except she had some children already, didn't have no man, and she was sure Pemberton was going to belong to her. Oh, she had a nerve. Come walking by any time of day she felt like it. Walked real slow in front of the house, looking. Never once spoke, not even a nod at me, unless Pemberton was home.

What kind of a fool did they think I was? I might have been heavy and clumsy, but I wasn't blind and crippled. I decided to see for myself what was what, and walked

4

I tell Pemberton all the time, some people just don't believe fat meat's greasy. Them's the kind of people you have to watch, let them know you mean business, or they walk on you like they walking on a cement sidewalk. Me and Pemberton done run this house a long time. We bought it at the beginning of the war, when everybody and his brother was going or coming, dying or buying, one or the other. We was supposed to be starting us a family and when that didn't work out, me and Pemberton thought we'd just as well rent the house out. Near about every year we fixed on it, put nice furniture in all the rooms, decent rugs on the floors. We take in mostly teachers because they don't keep up no noise, most of them, and they tend to their own business. That way you don't get riffraff.

This whole thing started when we give the kitchenette to a teacher named October Brown. I don't suspect Pemberton took to her when she first come in here. The chile was a little too much on the dark side for him to get excited about. Not that he would have turned down her money, he's black himself. Light skin may be upper-crust to him, but it don't mean nothin in my book. Let me tell you, I have known Thomas Pemberton to look twice at more than one high-yellow woman with good hair, and years ago, it near about cost him everything we had. But like I said, this thing with October Brown wasn't about how she looked. She wasn't nowhere near light skin, head hadn't been close to no straightening comb, either, woolly as a sheep's behind. Pitiful how young they start them teaching. She couldn't have been no more than twenty-one or two. "May I see Mr. Pemberton?" she asked us.

I tell him all the time about answering the door with no clothes on. Don't no well-to-do people answer the door in around to where the woman lived one day, strolled right up and knocked on her door. Don't you know Pemberton himself opened the door just like he lived there. You could have bought him for a penny. But did that stop him? No indeedy, he acted like he couldn't get enough of her.

Well. I'd done had enough of both of them. I took and set all Pemberton's clothes out by the trash for the ragman. Took his suits, his shirts, his shoes, everything. Put them in gunnysacks and set them right at the alley. He didn't know they was out there. That day he come home from work or wherever, and I told him just to go ahead on. If he wanted Mamie Turner so bad he had to sneak around with her while I was big with his baby, just go ahead on.

Oh, it was a mess. Needless to say, Pemberton got himself and his clothes together and crawled on back with me. He paid the price though. Reckon we both did. A couple of weeks later when the baby come here dead and no bigger than my hand, he blamed himself. Guess he felt like God was punishing him. Them was hard times for us.

I never heard what become of Mamie Turner. People talked. Said one of her boys belonged to Pemberton. He never said one way or the other, said just let it be. One thing for sure, he knew better than to bring some bastard child of that woman's in my face.

Later on, when we got this place and started to take in roomers, we made it clear that if you lived under our roof, wasn't going to be no foolishness. Professional people know the stakes, and we never allowed no one in here who wasn't decent. We done had preachers, railroad men, plus we had a few city workers come down from Topeka, mailmen and what not. After while, though, we said nothing but teachers.

"We don't have but two vacancies, but you can see the whole place, all five rooms," I told October Brown. Don't hurt for a new girl to see how the old ones keep theirs up. Right away she liked the kitchenette.

"Where are you staying now?" I asked her.

"I'm over at Reverend Jackson's in a double room," she said.

Reverend was a man of God, but from what I had heard, his place was high and wasn't too clean.

I told her, "I suspect me and Pemberton'll make up our minds and call over there directly."

So we did. We give October Brown the kitchenette. Teachers always saving up because they ain't got nothing to spend their money on unless they sending it home. Sure enough, October Brown said she would pay whatever we was charging.

"Generally our roomers get breakfast and supper," I told her. "Since you got the kitchenette your meals is extra. Saturdays y'all have to make do, or do without," I told her. And I give her all the rules about no smoking, no drinking, and no men. "You can see any men friends you want in the front room, but they can't go upstairs. This ain't that kind of house."

That was all right by her. Said she could get her own breakfast, which she must did, but I never smelled nothing coming out that kitchenette in the morning.

The day she moved in I had a Ruth Circle meeting at church. Pemberton and me ate early and I decided I'd fix a quick little supper for the roomers and set it out. Little buffet. Down she come and looked at the table.

"Help yourself to whatever you want," I said. I introduced her around the table so nobody could say I didn't see to it that they knew who she was. Jocelyn Jones was at Stowe, too. Mary Esther and tall, skinny Albertine Scott was at Attucks. Old Miss Dumas had done retired years ago, but she kept up with what was going on. October Brown sat down, and when they passed around the food, she put one spoonful of slaw on her plate. Nothing else. One spoonful of slaw.

"You ain't hungry?" Pemberton asked her.

Oh, she don't care for no conies and beans, Mr. Pemberton, she says, talking proper. But, she says, she'll just have a little bread and butter too, and be fine.

I could feel my mouth wanting to say something, but I didn't. When I was leaving out the house, I could hear the rest of them commence to sighing and fussing over what we was and what we wasn't having for supper. Pemberton wasn't no better. He likes to eat with the girls, carrying on about first one thing, then the other. They go on about coloreds and whites, about the school situation, the whites got this and that and we ain't. If it was left to Pemberton, I'd be fixing pies and cakes every day just so they could sit at the table and chew the cud longer.

Hadn't a month passed when a certain young man come sniffing around. Mr. Carter was good at fixing things and he used to help out Pemberton. Every year the two of them hung the storm windows up, but this particular day Carter was sick or something and sent over this boy he knew named James. They called him Shorty. James "Shorty" Wilson. Nice looking, about twenty-six or seven. Slick jitterbug. I don't know what went on between him and her, but I do know that James Shorty Boy got down off the ladder, come inside the house, and went up to October Brown's room, just as big. I had a fit. I told Pemberton he better get that boy out of there.

Well, Pemberton got him out. "We can't have no men upstairs. Now you git to gittin," Pemberton told him. "These is schoolteachers here," he said.

Shorty said, "Shoot, I didn't know that." Said his screwdriver was between the windows in one of the rooms and he just come in to get it in the kitchenette. But it got so every now and then, mostly now, he come by and sat right on the divan in the front room, talking to her.

Me and Pemberton didn't keep the place like a convent for the nuns, but we was on the good-house list for the school board all them years because we knew what they wanted for their teachers. Naturally if they lived with us, they walked the line. Pemberton always thought the girls would just catch on and do right. Not me. I don't know of no tale big enough to outdo what some of them teachers done tried one time or other. Truth was, most of them was careful. That chile October Brown, though, she wasn't no more careful than the sun is careful about coming up.

After while, I guess talking wasn't good enough for her and the fellow. Reverend's wife, Johnnie Mae, called up over here one day about some story she got from one of the women in her choir. The way she told it, she had seen October Brown with Shorty at Shady Maurice's joint out in the county. Said she was all over him, right out in the public. I wanted to ask Johnnie Mae what the woman was doing out there herself.

Pemberton walked around here talking about "Now, Lydia, you don't know for sure. You was a girl once yourself," he said. "Don't hurt to have at least one boy to flirt around with."

"You the one said he was too old for her," I said, but Pemberton swore he didn't know nothing. Pemberton could be slick when he wanted to. He was the same man took me all the way to St. Louis without so much as a cricket's twitch to my daddy about it. I called her downstairs. "Miss October Brown!"

She come runnin to the top of the steps.

"What is it? What's the matter?" she said.

"Could you come downstairs for a minute, please? Won't take but a minute."

She come down. The three of us sat in the front room. Pemberton sat on the divan not saying nothing. He says I lit into her, but I say I just told her what was what.

"We been keeping teachers for a long time, so I know what I'm talking about. We been hearing stories, about you and a young man being at that honky-tonk joint out in the county. I don't know if you know it or not, but that ain't no place for a teacher to be seen. People don't want no woman running around at night and teaching their children in the daytime. School board don't like it either. We don't want nobody in here going to mess us up with the board. So we don't want to hear no more about it. That's all. I just thought I'd tell you."

The rat can't call the cat to account, so when October Brown got through looking big-eyed at me, she tied up her housecoat and went on back up the steps to her room. Pemberton went back to the kitchen grumbling about what people is bound to do and what I can't put a stop to.

A couple of Sundays went by. The girls was all nicey-nicey to each other. They come up with the idea that all of them ought to go together to hear Mary Esther and Albertine sing their duet on Reverend Jackson's anniversary program. Jocelyn usually went to Gethsemane and took October Brown with her, but this time they said they'd go hear Mary Esther and those at Strangers Rest. That's me and Pemberton's church, so naturally me and Pemberton went too.

We sat all in one row—Pemberton, me, October Brown, Jocelyn Jones, and Miss Dumas. Albertine and Mary Esther ain't even up there yet when the door opens and a few more folks come in and start finding their seats. Well before Pemberton could get his glasses on good I hunched him so hard he near about dropped them. It was Shorty James Wilson, all right, coming down the aisle with what must have been his wife on his arm, because I don't know no man who would sport a woman fixing to have a baby if she didn't belong to him. His wife was big too, seven months at least. Now I'm sitting right next to October Brown, watching this. I could feel the little jerk she made when she saw them. Blood went right out of her face. You never would've thought it, though, if you hadn't have seen it. She folded her hands in her lap, calm as a stone, and commenced to watch the whole program.

It wasn't my place to say nothing. I suspect she always knew he was married. But now, in front of everybody, she could see for herself what the man cared about. He was coming to church with his family. She wasn't no more to him than a hot time on a Saturday night. I could have warned her about men acting a fool when their wife is big, but you always got to keep the right space between you and the people that live in your house, or else you borrowing trouble.

I gave October Brown credit for cutting Shorty off quick, not wasting a day replacing him. Seems like the same Sunday even, she started parting her hair different, putting in some hot curls for a change. Spent near about all her time sewing new skirts and such. Biggest thing, she took to going out Saturday nights. Since Jocelyn went with her, and they wasn't out too late, I figured the girls was having some clean fun. You should have heard them, "How I look in this?" "How you like that?" Regular dolls couldn't have been more prissy. I knew a man was in it somewhere.

Whoever he was, October Brown kept it to herself. She didn't want to speak too soon, I thought. Lordy, she swooned and carried on around here.

Tickled me watching her. I figured he was somebody up in Topeka somewhere, because I noticed she started packing up a lunch each time, probably to take on the bus. Keeping it all away from the house was smart. The girls whispered and peeped, but she didn't give them nothing to chew on. It got so, most Saturdays she went out early, come back Sundays. Sometimes she'd up and disappear on a Wednesday night too.

Deep in the wintertime, I hate going out. It was coming up to my birthday and the girls told me, said I ought to get my hair done. Every year they took me to the teachers' banquet at the YWCA. I didn't care how good Mattie Donald could do hair, I wasn't going to no beauty parlor in the snow. Well, October Brown said she would do it. She said she used to do her auntie's hair all the time. Looking at hers, I wouldn't have guessed it, but I said okay. Couldn't hurt.

Generally, I didn't make a habit of going up to the girls' rooms except once or twice a year to take a look-see or to fix up. I must say, October Brown had done hers pretty. On the table, under the radio, she had laid a little shawl with the fringe, put little lamps and what-nots all around. Crocheted doilies on her armchair. Real pale, blue chenille spread that went with the wallpaper. Right nice.

"Come on in, Miss Lydia," she said. I thought I smelled cloves and I saw orange slices floating in a double boiler of black tea on the burner. I'd done took off my apron and put on the sweater the girls got me for Christmas.

"Don't you look nice," she said, buttering me up. She sat me down in her big armchair, unpinned my braids, and commenced to let all my hair loose.

"I wish *I* had good hair," she said. "I like your silver-gray, just like spun silk around the edges," she said.

My old gray head looking like spun silk.

"You want to take off your earrings?"

I told her no indeedy, Pemberton bought me them gold hoops off a gypsy man over in Missouri one time. Besides my ring, they was the onliest jewelry I ever had.

"I'm going to give you a hot-oil treatment first," she said.

Lord knows I didn't need no grease in my hair.

"It'll loosen up all the old skin on your scalp," she said.

I told her I was old all over, wasn't enough grease in the world to help that.

"Aw, you aren't that old," she said. "I'll bet if Mr. Pemberton wasn't around, the men would still be chasing you. You must have had your pick before you married him," she said.

"Well, I used to could hold my own," I told her.

Truth was I never had a lot of men coming after me, but I got the one I wanted. While she messed around with my hair, I told her about how Pemberton took me from my papa's house in St. Joe and brought me to see Kansas City for the first time. Every life got a little sweet in it, and them were sweet days. Me and Pemberton was young and looking for life. Hadn't even figured out yet that we was livin it. I reckon if Pemberton's daddy's boss man hadn't needed somebody to drive his car to his son in Kansas City, we never woulda got here. Laid back in October Brown's chair, thinking about that time, I'd got so lost I didn't notice how she had done stuck a pillow behind my neck and put a little stool up under my feet. She was working my scalp with her fingers. Near about put me to sleep.

After while she got me up and put me on my knees on a pillow in her straight-back chair at the sink. First off, she did the castile wash. Then she had to use the coconut oil soap. Then vinegar water to cut that. Then it was egg whites for the protein. Lord, when my knees give out she said we was only halfway through. After the egg whites, it was cold water. Then hot water. Then warm water. Then rose water. Finally, she wrapped my head in a towel she had warming close to the burners. She sat me in the arm-chair again, parted my hair, and wiped water till I was dead sleep. I'd done laid back and drifted a long time while she fixed around at the icebox.

"Did you ever have any children, Miss Lydia?" she asked.

"Naw, I didn't. Tried two, three times, but none of them made it. Must not have been meant to have them," I said.

"That's too bad," she said, frowning.

"It's all happened so long ago, I done forgot."

She changed the subject. "We might as well have a little party while we wait for your hair to dry," she said. She set us out some tiny tea cups with flowers all over them and gold at the edges. Laid out a nice little plate of deviled eggs. I don't generally eat deviled eggs in the wintertime, but they was good with the saltines.

"You done already started you a nice life teaching. Think you gonna quit one of these days, raise you some children yourself?"

What did I want to say that for? All of a sudden she stopped chewing and got right up from her chair. Before she could get her face hid she tuned up. Eyes got all big and watery.

"What's the matter, honey? Couldn't be bad as all that. What's the trouble?"

She put her hand up for me to hush, so I did. I waited while she went to the bureau and got a handkerchief to wipe her eyes.

"I think I've done what you asked," she said. " I mean, I've been very discreet, have I not?"

If she was talking about running around and such she was on the mark.

"Yes," I told her. "You been quiet far as this house is concerned."

"Well, now I think I'm going to have to ask you to bear with me."

"For what? This sounds like something I don't want to hear."

"Well, I've gotten myself into a big bind."

"How big?" I asked her. "Don't tell me you done gone and got yourself in trouble."

Well, of course then she didn't say anything. Just wiped her tears.

"Is that it? You're in trouble with the boy? Don't tell me you're pregnant."

That was it, all right. I swear, when I get to heaven, I'm going to ask the Lord why it is that some women can have babies as easy as they shell peas, and others can't have none, no matter how hard they try.

13

I told her, I said, "I know my timing ain't too keen, but I told you long time ago me and Pemberton is very careful about stuff like this."

She kept on wiping her eyes and nodding her head yes.

"Well, now the first thing you got to do is you got to be sure the people uptown don't get wind of this. Maybe we can keep you, but only till you figure out what you going to do. Maybe we can hold off a month or so."

"Oh, would you?" she says.

"I'd have to talk it out with Pemberton. Excuse me for saying it, but you ain't in no position to have a baby right now," I told her. I knew too many women done worked it out quietly and nobody was the wiser, but that was between her and the boy.

"Well, what's the boy saying? He want to get married, or what?" I asked her.

She went to crying again. "James says he just needs some more time."

"Wait a minute," I said. "James? What James?"

She commenced to looking like a lamb scared of the shears.

"I thought you knew," she said. "I thought . . ."

I'll never understand how she could have held her mouth to let it fall out. The whole thing come clear to me then. It was James Shorty Wilson she'd been seeing all this time. After all that, she'd done played out a plan to get that man away from his wife, and I'd done sat by and let her do it right in my face.

Hairdo or no, I couldn't get out of her room fast enough. But not before I had a little piece of my say to her.

I said, "I should have known. You come in here looking all lost and asking for help, I should have known from the first. Oh, wasn't you smart, come fixing my hair and Oh Miss Lydia ain't we prettying me, sewing them short dresses so you can get that man away from his wife. You must've thought you was cute taking him out of town where nobody could see till you got his nose open good. What did you do? Soak your bloody rag in his coffee? Bake your nappy hair in his cake? Guess that wasn't enough, so you had to go and get yourself pregnant. Well, let me tell you something, you'll not sit your black self up in my house and grin about how you did it, not if I can help it. Shame on you, girl. Shame on the mamma that raised you."

Evil knows where evil sleeps. If she thought she could sneak around and help herself to a man that wasn't hers, she had another thought coming. Me and Pemberton knew the law and if we wanted her out, she had to go. I couldn't cook a pot of water, couldn't eat a crumb until I wrote out the letter me and Pemberton was going to give her.

February 18, 1952

Dear Miss October Brown,

This is to tell you that by February 25, 1952, you have to vacate your kitchenette at 5116 Wynona Ave., Kansas City, Kansas. Our rules say we only rent to upstanding single women with no children. If you are not gone by then, we will take further action.

Yours truly,
Lydia Pemberton, Thomas Pemberton
Proprietors

That evening Pemberton come in ready for his bath. While he run water in the tub, he took off his shirt and throwed it on the bed. That's when he saw the letter.

"What's this?" he said. He knows I don't generally leave mail laying around like that.

"We going to have to put October Brown out," I said. I commenced to tell Pemberton all of what I'd done got out of October Brown that evening. Pemberton was shocked, all right. He shook his head and went on in the bathroom. I suspect he sat in the tub over an hour. I know the news got him because he whistled low like he do when something

Maxine Clair

big is on his mind.

He come out the bathroom and put on his robe, said he wasn't going to eat with the girls that evening. Had him one helping of limas and little bitty piece of corn bread. That was all. He sat in the front room and read the paper while me and the girls ate. Course October Brown didn't come down at all.

That night all that nervous quietness in the house must have woke me up. Must have been two or three in the morning—Pemberton sleeps sound like he's dead except he'll turn over every now and then—I woke up and he was laying on his back with his eyes wide open like he's sure enough dead. I hunched him.

"Lyddy," he says, he don't even blink. "Don't you think we ought to just stay out of the whole thing? Let October Brown keep her room till the school year is out or least till she has a chance to figure out what's what? They's bound to let her go at the school, and she's bound to go back to Ohio to her people. And if by some big miracle, she don't get fired, she still got to go to her people, just later on probably. Seem like we ought to keep her till then."

Poor Pemberton. He don't think straight sometimes.

"The word's going to get around, Pemberton, then what? Come next fall guess what house ain't going to be on the list?"

"Lyddy, there's always somebody looking for a place to stay."

"Go on back to sleep," I said. "See how you feel in the morning."

By the time morning come, look like Pemberton got back his cheerful self. Woke me up, kissing me on my neck and fumbling around, talking about how we was young as we felt like being. If I hadn't had to get up and start breakfast, I might have took him up on showing me just how young he thought we was. Me and him had us a good ole breakfast of grits and ham before anybody stirred upstairs.

16

He sopped up his gravy, then he opened up the subject of what to do with October Brown.

"You know, Lydia, the chile is in a fix. If Johnnie Mae Jackson catches wind of anything, you know Reverend Jackson ain't going to take her in over there. No private family we know will take her, either. I been thinking about this all night," he said. "God moves in mysterious ways, his wonders to perform, am I right? Don't it strike you as peculiar that October Brown come to this door, *our* door, *we* the ones who took her in. Now here she is bringing a child into the world under our roof. Don't that seem funny to you?"

It seemed like a shame to me is what it seemed, but Pemberton had done cooked up a whole new life for everybody, including me, and I wanted to hear about it.

"Now I know the other roomers wouldn't like it, yet and still wouldn't it be something having a baby around here squealing. If it was downstairs, wouldn't be no trouble. Me and you both home practically every day. We got the one empty room off the kitchen don't nobody usually want. What if by some streak of luck—not that she deserves it—but say October Brown could save her job, just till the end of the year, which is right around the corner. Next term, maybe they'll hire her over in Missouri. A little child needs a decent place, and that's just what we got here."

I could see wasn't no messing around with Pemberton no longer. He'd done gone clear off with it, like I was just talking to hear myself. Evidently he couldn't understand how bound and determined I was. It was the principle. Without another word I went straight into the bedroom and got the letter, put it square in front of him on the table and give him the ink pen. "Sign it, Pemberton," I said.

He looked up at me like I had an extra head on my shoulders. "You been knowing me almost my whole life," I said. "You ought to know as long as I'm living and breathing, I'm not having no bastard child under my roof.

October Brown might do fine, but not in my house."

Pemberton left the letter laying on the table. He moped and scoped around a while. Next day he told me, said, "All right, Lydia. I guess you got a right to grow old in a quiet place if you want to. But we ain't going to put her out yet. She's going to stay here till the summertime, unless she gets married, or goes back to Ohio or something. We can't kick her out into the street. It ain't right."

"You still got it wrong, Pemberton," I told him. "She ain't staying a minute past Thursday."

"Naw now, Lydia. You done got your way about everything else so just let it alone. The girl is going to stay here till her job is out or they fire her. Ain't no need in us putting no more stumbling blocks up for her."

I never seen Pemberton so stubborn about somebody else's business.

"Pemberton," I said. "I'm going to tell you this one more time. First place, she ain't no girl, not no more. Second place, she ain't no decent woman. And number three, I don't want her here and that's the end of it."

With all the commotion the next couple of days, I knew she was going. By Saturday she'd done brought in orange crates and newspaper. She cooked up there in her room and her and Jocelyn ate up there. Mary Esther was big-eyed and teary every night at the table.

You might know Albertine done figured out some of it. "I don't see why October Brown wants to move closer to the school. There isn't a nicer place up there, unless of course she's not saying what else is going on," she said.

But Pemberton, he was the one acted a pure-D-fool. Friday night I fixed him some greens, baked a whole ham, candied up some sweet potatoes and cut up a little onion and tomato like he likes. If he touched a crumb my name ain't Lydia. He put on his coat just as big and drove the car over to the dinette. I know because he come back in here with a pig foot sandwich. Sat right up in my face and ate it without saying a word.

I told him, "Mister, you mess around and both of y'all going to be eating pig feet together somewhere, you embarrass me like that in front of the roomers again. You can act a fool if you want to, but it don't change nothing."

He went on in the room. I looked at him sitting on the bed. We was both getting old. We didn't have no business fighting. First thing you know, people would be talking about *us*. I didn't know what got into Pemberton, but I wasn't going to let that girl mess over us.

That Monday, Pemberton went fishing. Like he didn't want to be around. Came back with a whole mess of croakers I cleaned and fried. He ate and never said a word.

Wednesday come, he sat right at the other end of the table and ate his breakfast. Didn't say nothing, but he ate. Got right up and left out. I heard the truck leave and figured he was gone to the plant. When he come in, he had a sack from the hardware place. Took it up and set it outside October Brown's door. Then left outside and was gone the whole rest of the day.

October Brown and Jocelyn come in with more crates and newspaper, flitting and flying around most of the evening. Pemberton went up and down a few times with the hammer or a screwdriver, helping them.

Thursday came and nobody come down for breakfast. Mary Esther and Albertine both said they didn't have time. Old Miss Dumas didn't want nothing but hot water and lemon. Pemberton swallowed a sausage and biscuit and went right on upstairs. I figured it must be moving day because October Brown and Jocelyn stayed home. With Pemberton helping, they pushed around the furniture, talked, and carried on like they was kin. I got out my embroidery and sat in the front room.

About ten in the morning, Pemberton loaded some stuff in the truck and left out. I hadn't heard where October Brown was moving to. Next thing, Pemberton pulled up in front of the house, and Mr. Carter was riding with him. October Brown came down first, wearing pants, hair tied up in a bandanna, carrying a crate full of linens. Pemberton come in, went on back in the bedroom, and closed the door.

Look like October Brown carried more stuff out than she brought when she came. Her and Jocelyn made ten or twelve trips carting stuff together. Passed by the front room like I was a chair sitting there. Carter stayed outdoors in the truck, fixing the stuff in the back so it wouldn't fall. Finally I guess they was through because they didn't come back in. When the truck didn't leave, I looked out the window. All three of them—October Brown, Jocelyn, and Mr. Carter—was standing there, leaning against the truck, looking at the house. Then, lo and behold, here comes Pemberton out the bedroom with our old suitcase in his hand and a armful of clothes. He come on through the front room, didn't say a word. Went out the door.

First I thought he looked right silly, call himself going somewhere with one suitcase and two or three changes of clothes. Then when he banged around trying to open the door, I thought he was acting like a spoiled child trying to get his way. I decided to teach him. Let him go ahead on.

The picture I can see clear is Pemberton in the back of the truck, and Mr. Carter driving, pulling off with October Brown and Jocelyn up front. Pemberton sitting on a crate with his elbows on his knees like he's sitting on the toilet. Got on his good shirt and Sunday shoes, riding up the street.

Jocelyn came back, but Pemberton didn't. Not yet. Reverend Jackson is letting them stay over there. I imagine Johnnie Mae is having a time with that. Of all people, she's on Pemberton's side about the principle of the thing. They can keep their principle. Pemberton'll be back. He acts a fool sometimes, but he'll be back.

BATHING MOTHER

MILENA MILANI

Milena Milani was born in Savona, Italy. A writer and fine artist, she was educated in Rome, where she later settled.

Ms. Milani has exhibited her art work, featuring a unique combination of painting-and-text and ceramics-and-text, in one-woman shows throughout Italy. She is also a prolific writer, the author of several novels, a volume of poetry, a collection of short stories, and three volumes of essays. In 1982 the city of Milan awarded her its Gold Medal of Civic Merit for her rich contributions to literature, poetry, and the arts. She was awarded the honorary title of Grande Ufficiale al stata nominata della Repubblica Italiana by Francesco Cossiga in 1988.

The following selection, originally published in Italian as "Madre al bagno," first appeared in the collection *Pagine come gocce.*

Ms. Milani currently lives in Rome.

My mother sat waiting for me in bed propped up by two pillows. She was embroidering a doily with the colored floss that I had brought her. Even in the hospital she could not sit without doing anything. When I arrived she was finishing a flower, its five petals opening wide; then she said she wanted to go to the lavatory where there was also a bathtub.

"Before eating I would like to wash," she said mildly, with a little girl's smile.

I agreed, even though I was worried that she might catch cold. I had her get into the wheelchair so she would not get tired, and she sat there, regal in the beautiful white-and-blue dressing gown that I had bought her in Paris. I wheeled her through the wide corridor that divided the wards, and as we moved along my mother kept greeting nurses passing on either side, and even some people who were on their way to visit patients.

"You know them all?" I asked her.

She said she did, as she had been in the hospital for such a long time. I acted as if I believed her, and she was relieved that I left it at that.

When she had first arrived at the hospital, my mother had been happy. In all the years of her life she had never been ill. This was her first time. And now finally, she could have a rest. "I can't just stay in bed though, sleeping, being waited on. I'll get bored if I don't do anything. My legs are tired, but not my hands. Bring me something to embroider."

So I had found those doilies that had borders of colorful garland designs, in which you had to embroider even the scallop shapes. My mother was excited. "How will I do those flowers, and the leaves." She had chosen skeins of light blue satiny cotton floss, a lively red, and even a golden yellow. Restless but patient, she forged ahead with her work.

The woman in the bed to her left (on the right side was the wall) had asked her why she was working body and soul. Mother had answered: "We have so much time on our hands here, one has to fill up those empty hours somehow."

Now as I took her to the bath she was tingling with excitement.

"Did you bring the towel, did you bring the sponge and the soap?" she kept asking.

I answered, yes, I had brought everything, that it was all in the pouch that hung from the backrest of the wheelchair. We arrived at that horrible room that was always a mess, with water on the floor, hair in the sink, leaking faucets, cracked mirrors. I had to pretend that everything was perfect and the way it should be, that she was going to have a marvelous bath.

Fortunately the poorly lit room was empty. A dim light bulb hung high up on a wire, and the tub was one of those in which you had to sit. Before taking my mother into the cubicle, I tried to scrub the enamel, which had yellowish stains that would not come clean.

"Hurry up," my mother said, "someone might come, and then there'll be a line."

But no one came. I helped my mother get out of the wheelchair and then undress. Her naked white body moved me. I had come out of that belly. It seemed impossible—she was hairless like a little girl who still has to grow up, who knows nothing of the world or of life.

The breasts that had fed me hung empty on her chest. In one of them was nesting the evil that had befallen her, and on the skin were blue spots where the cobalt had touched.

"Mother!" I wanted to shout, but instead I told her that the water was just right and that she could get into the tub.

Carefully she climbed over the edge and sat down, and I began washing her back. She pressed her legs and feet together and with one hand clung to the outer rim. "Rub hard; you're not hurting me."

I soaped and scrubbed her back up and down, and she was ecstatic. Then with the mobile showerhead I rinsed away the foam with a jet of warm water until her back was smooth and rosy. I did the same in front, my hand sliding carefully over her, over my sick mother for whom, according to science and medicine, there was no hope. I washed her and I prayed.

"Don't let her die," I begged God, but his answer did not reach my ears. My mind in confusion, I was about to burst into tears.

My mother on the other hand was smiling, congratulating me on the good job I was doing. Suddenly she asked: "Did you bring a clean blouse?" I helped her out of the tub, checking to see if she was cold (I felt her feet, one of them with the broken and twisted nail crushed so many years ago), and dried her and sprinkled her with talcum powder. With a blissful sigh she tried to help, saying: "You know, I feel fine. I think I'm cured."

I agreed with her. This always happens after a bath. The skin breathes freely, the pores drink in oxygen, every creature is cleansed of the filth of the earth, restored and ready for what fate has in store. As if she had guessed my thoughts, my mother added:

"If I get called, at least I know I'll be fresh and clean." She smiled as if to say: "I won't be caught by surprise; I want to go in style."

She returned to the wheelchair, and before we faced the corridor once more I combed her hair. She wanted her pearl earrings. Her hair was light and sparse; it had become like bird's down. She touched it and said:

"They told me this would happen, but I could always buy myself a wig."

She added cheerfully that she wanted an ash-blond one, like her hair before the treatments had started. "With thick curls," she specified, "and a part on the side."

We set off on our way back, wheeling through the

corridor, the aromas of lunch filling the air with anticipation.

"I'm going to have some minestrone," my mother said. "I don't want pasta with sauce."

Her bed neighbor was struggling with spaghetti, but for my mother there was just a bowl with bits of canary-yellow pasta. It was on the bedside table, already cold. She tried a spoonful, but she had lost her appetite.

"I think I'll be getting back to my embroidery," she said, taking the doily and threading a long sky-blue strand into the needle without using her glasses.

I watched her, and felt my heart grieve.

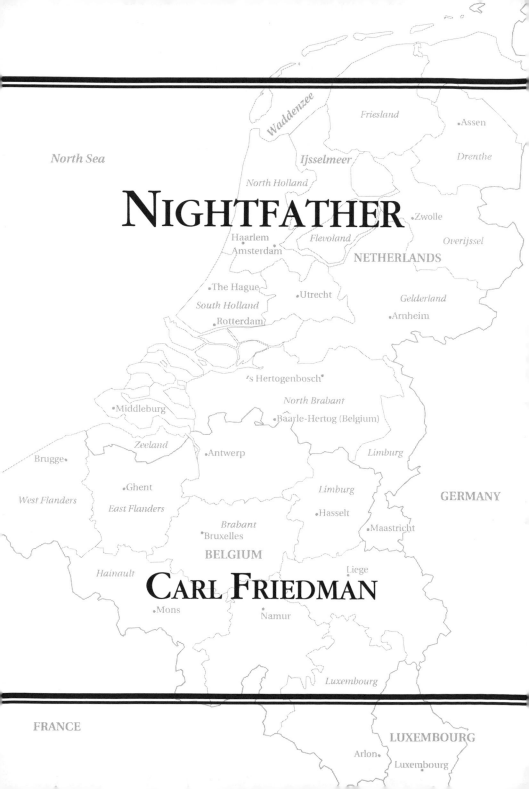

NIGHTFATHER

CARL FRIEDMAN

© Marijke Kunkeler

Carl Friedman was born in Eindhoven, The Netherlands. After spending a significant portion of her life in Antwerp, Belgium, in 1977 she returned to The Netherlands.

A translator, journalist, poet, and novelist, she has had her work published in major Dutch literary magazines. The following selection is an excerpt from her forthcoming novel *Nightfather*, to be published in September by Persea Books. The book was originally published in The Netherlands in 1991 and subsequently in Germany. Ms. Friedman has lectured widely to students in both countries concerning it.

Ms. Friedman now lives in Amsterdam, raising her son and working on her second novel.

Camp

He never mentions it by name. It might have been Trebibor or Majdawitz, Soblinka or Birkenhausen. He talks about "the camp" as if there had been just one.

"After the war," he says, "I saw a film about the camp. With prisoners frying an egg for breakfast." He slaps his forehead with the palm of his hand. "An egg!" he says shrilly. "In the camp!"

So camp is somewhere where no one fries eggs.

Camp is not so much a place as a condition. "I've had camp," he says. That makes him different from us. We've had chicken pox and German measles. And after Simon fell out of a tree, he got a concussion and had to stay in bed for weeks.

But we've never had camp.

Most of the time he drops the past participle for convenience. Then he says, "I have camp," as if the situation hadn't changed. And it's true, it hasn't. He still has camp, especially in his face. Not so much in his nose or his ears, although they're big enough, but in his eyes.

I saw a wolf in the zoo once, with eyes like that. He was pacing back and forth in his cage, up and down and up and down, to the front and back again. I spent a long time staring at him through the bars.

Full of worry, I went to look for Max and Simon. They were hanging over the railings around the monkey rock, laughing at a baboon throwing pebbles.

"Please, come and look at the wolf," I said, but they weren't interested. Only when I started to cry did Max reluctantly turn away and follow me.

"Well?" he said in a bored voice when we were standing in front of the wolf's cage. "What's the matter with him?"

"He has camp!" I sobbed. Max glanced through the bars.

"Impossible," he said. "Wolves don't get camp."

Then he pulled me by the hand. I had to go back to the monkeys with him.

When we got home and my mother saw my tear-stained cheeks, she asked what had made me unhappy. Max shrugged.

"She isn't big enough yet for the zoo."

Nice

Max is drinking from a puddle. He's lying flat in the mud, sucking the brown water up through a straw.

"What does it taste like?" we ask impatiently. But he shuts his eyes contemptuously and goes on sucking.

"You little pig!" my mother calls from afar. "You'll make yourself sick!"

We have to go inside, even Simon and I, although we haven't had our turn at tasting yet.

During the night, Max complains of feeling sick. He clutches his stomach and groans, "I must have swallowed worms. I can feel them wriggling!"

You don't get camp from drinking muddy water. You don't get camp from playing outside without your coat on, or from never washing your hands. I don't know how or why my father got camp. Maybe he got it because he's different from most of the people I know. Because he's different, my mother is different, too. And because the two of them are different, Max, Simon, and I are different from ordinary children. At home you don't notice it, but at school you do.

"A man flying through the air!" The teacher smiles as

she bends over my drawing.

"He isn't flying," I tell her, "he's hanging. See, he's dead, his tongue is blue. And these prisoners have to look at him as a punishment. My father is there, too. Here, he's the one with the big ears."

"That's nice," says the teacher.

"It's not," I say. "They're starving and now they have to wait a long time for their soup." But she's already moved on to the next desk.

"Two pixies on a toadstool," she calls out, clapping her hands. "That's really nice!"

In a rage I make great scrawls across my drawing and turn the paper over. What's so nice about a couple of pixies? I draw a whole lot more than two: five in the snow and one on top of the watchtower.

Roll Call

He doesn't have camp only in his face but in his fingers, too. They often drum nervously on the edge of the table or on the arms of his chair.

And he has camp in his feet. In the middle of the night his feet slide out of bed, carrying him down the stairs and through the hallway. We can hear him far away, opening and closing doors, without ever finding the peace he's looking for behind any of them.

"Were you on the prowl again last night?" my mother asks when we are at breakfast. He nods. She puts her hand over his. "Ephraim," she says, "Ephraim."

Sometimes his prowling wakes us up. Then we go downstairs in our pajamas to keep him company. He walks around in circles while we watch him from the sofa. When my mother comes in, he stops.

"I'm keeping you all up," he mumbles. She rubs her eyes and sighs.

"Never mind," she says. "You're alive, that's what counts. You can dance on the roof all night as far as I'm concerned.".

He bends over her and she nudges her forehead into the hollow at the bridge of his nose. Their faces fit together like a jigsaw puzzle.

One night Simon and I are wakened by loud thumps. Together we go to see what's happening. The landing light is on. We stand on the cold linoleum, blinking in the glare. The door to the main bedroom is open. My father is lying on the floor inside. His eyebrow is bleeding. Max and my mother are kneeling beside him.

"You take his other arm," my mother says, "otherwise he'll fall against the closet again."

They pull him to his feet. As soon as he's up, he jumps to attention and brings his hand to his head.

"Caps off," he whispers in German. He lets his arm drop to his side, then jerks it up again. "Caps on." There's blood on his fingers.

"No, Ephraim." My mother takes him by the shoulders. Max skips around the two of them like a puppy.

"The bell for roll call has rung," says my father in a voice I don't recognize.

"There isn't any bell here," my mother says, pushing him toward the bed. "You're home with me."

When he's sitting on the edge of the bed, she turns around without letting him go and says, "It's all right, go back to bed now."

Deep down under the covers I start to cry.

"Don't be frightened," says Simon. "It isn't real. Papa's been dreaming everything, the bell and the roll call."

"And the blood?" I ask him from under the blankets. "Did he dream that, too?"

There is no reply.

The SS

My mother is busy sticking a piece of cardboard up over the sink. She has written "BRUSH YOUR TEETH!" on it in big red letters. I'm especially impressed by the exclamation mark.

"That's the way to tell the children," says my father in a mocking voice. He's standing in the doorway to the bathroom, his hands in his pockets.

"Decent shoes and good teeth are the pillars of society," my mother says.

"Maybe so, but do you really have to put up signs on the wall?"

"If I feel like it," says my mother defensively.

"Maybe you'll feel like putting up a few more tomorrow, in German, with, say, 'Bath and Disinfection' or 'It Is Your Duty to Keep Clean!'"

"Don't be like that," says my mother. She pulls the cardboard off the wall and walks away.

"Well?" he says, turning to me. "Shouldn't you be brushing you teeth? *Schnell!*" He laughs.

"It was such a good sign," I say gravely, squeezing some toothpaste onto my brush. By way of belated homage, I give all my teeth an extra good brushing.

When I've rinsed my mouth, I turn to see my father pacing up and down on the landing. "When the SS felt bored," he says, "they'd pick a prisoner at random, take off his cap, and fling it up high onto the barbed wire. 'Go fetch your cap,' they'd shout, 'or you'll get a bullet in the back!'"

I nod. Barefooted, I go to the bedroom. Simon is staying at a friend's. His bed is scarily empty. Max is allowed to stay up late because he's the oldest. The moment I'm under the blankets, my father's head appears around the door.

"But the barbed wire was electrified," he says. "It takes the SS to dream up something like that."

Though my mother has tucked me in, I can't fall asleep. I go and sit on Simon's bed, by the window. Gently I push the curtains apart. It's windy outside. Clouds with dragons' backs are chasing one another across the sky. Max says that space is infinite and that there are too many stars to count. Even if you spent your entire life counting them, not eating or sleeping or going to the bathroom, you still wouldn't ever reach the end.

I sit on Simon's bed and look at the sky. The black is blacker than usual. I'm almost sucked up into it. Max says that when it's night here, it's daytime somewhere else in the world. But what's the use of that? It takes the SS to dream up a thing like that. And the bit about the **stars, too.**

Eichmann

"What a funny father you have," Nellie says, giggling. She looks at me expectantly, but I avoid her eyes. What can I say? She knows nothing about hunger or about the SS. Words like *barracks*, *latrine*, or *crematorium* mean nothing to her. She speaks a different language.

Nellie's father doesn't have camp, he has a bicycle that he rides to the factory, with a lunch box strapped to the carrier.

Her mother wears checkered carpet slippers all the time. She skates along, up and down the kitchen, scarcely lifting her feet from the floor. The kitchen is where she lives, between the dirty dishes and her mending. She looks permanently angry, not just at us but at the pans, at the coffee pot, and at the whole world. Her false teeth lie in a little bowl on the drainboard. She only puts them in on Sundays, when she goes to church.

"You have a television, don't you?" she says when I come around to the back door after school to ask if Nellie is in. "Then you'll be watching Eichmann, too." The hostility in her voice makes me nervous. I fix my gaze on the doormat. "Don't you know who Eichmann is?"

She skates back and forth angrily. Along the way she noisily pushes a chair under the table and fiddles with the knobs on the stove.

"The man's an animal! They were right to put him in a glass cage. I'd like to kick him to death, that dirty bastard!" She takes a long time wiping her hands on her apron. "We saw it for ourselves on television yesterday. All the Jews were pushed into a truck and, as they were being driven off, the gas came on inside. Everybody choked to death. There was a little puppy dog running around making whimpering noises. They flung that poor little thing into the truck, too."

She raises her arms to show how it was done, but bumps into a closet.

"Your brain just refuses to take it in!" she says, her toothless mouth wide open. "What harm could a puppy dog do? A little puppy like that isn't Jewish, is he?" Nellie appears, making faces behind her mother's back.

"Hello! Let's go out and play."

"No," I say. "No, I have to get home."

My socks are sliding down, but I don't stop. When I rush into our living room, the television is on. I can see the glass cage on the screen. There's a bald man with eyeglasses sitting in it. He's talking into a microphone. He doesn't look like an animal, he looks like Mr. Klerk, who sometimes substitutes for our teacher, and who makes us sing *Oh, lovely flowers, sleep ye still?* at the beginning of the lesson.

"Is that Eichmann?" I say, disappointed. "He doesn't look horrible at all, he looks like Mr. Klerk from our school." My father nods.

"He looks like the mailman or the baker. The mailman delivers letters and the baker bakes bread and Eichmann sent masses of people to the gas chamber. He just did his job as others do theirs. It makes you sick."

"Then why are you watching?"

35

"Because I want to understand. But I understand it less now than I did then."

"Nellie's mother says she'd like to kick him to death." My father laughs.

"With those worn-out slippers of hers?"

He lights a cigarette.

"There are lots of people who'd like to do that," he says. "The papers are full of it: letters sent in by people offering to kill Eichmann. Now that he's defenseless, now that anyone can crush him under the toe of an old slipper. A whole army of volunteers. Where were those heroes when we needed them? I find that much harder to understand now than ever."

Woods

My father has bought a secondhand car. It's a red Austin with a black roof and a black hood. It has a friendly look with its bulbous front, like those cars in animated cartoons that can think and speak. "That isn't a car," the children in the street tease, "it's a coffee grinder!"

"You should have bought an Opel," says our neighbor's son.

"My father doesn't buy anything German," Max mumbles. I don't know why he's ashamed.

On Sunday morning my father takes Simon and me for a ride. The sky is blue, and we sit in the back seat. My father drives us to a duck pond outside town. There's a bridge over the water there. We stand on the bridge and drop stale bread through the railings.

Later on, we just drive around, along sandy country roads, past fields full of dusty cows. My father is humming. Suddenly he slows down. He leans his head toward the windshield and brakes. On the right side of the road there's a ditch and, beyond that, a narrow, overgrown path leading away.

"Great woods," he says. We nod. He clicks his tongue. "Great woods to escape into. So thick and so deep. They'd never find you there, not the slightest chance."

He gets out. We stay where we are and watch him jump across the ditch. Then the woods swallow him up.

"What's he up to?" Simon wonders nervously.

"The usual," I say, "just a little escaping." Simon winds down the window.

"I can't hear a thing. Only birds."

"You can't hear escaping," I whisper. "Escaping has to be done very quietly, otherwise it doesn't work."

"And what about us?" he says.

I start sucking my thumb. What does Simon know about such things? Far away, hidden by all that foliage, my father is running. There are twigs and beetles in his hair. Perhaps he won't come back until after dark, his clothes torn. "Great woods!" he will say, sweaty and out of breath.

But here he is already. He isn't even panting.

"For you," he says. He sticks a handful of blackberries through the window.

"Lucky they didn't find you," I sigh, as he gets ready to start the car. He looks around in surprise.

"Who?"

Scouts

On Wednesday afternoons Nellie doesn't come to play. That's when she goes to Brownies. Right after lunch, she puts on her uniform. I don't like the skirt or the blouse, but the socks are lovely: They have a tassel on the side.

When Nellie is dressed in her uniform she looks different and behaves differently.

"Look," I point. I've drawn circles with crayon on my spinning top, and when the top is spun hard, the circles merge together.

"I don't have time right now," says Nellie, "I've got to go to Brownies." In passing she kicks my top into the gutter.

"What are you going to do there?" I call, running after her. She turns around and shrugs.

"Sing songs, tracking, all sorts of things. You should ask your mother to let you join too, it costs next to nothing."

"May I join Brownies?" I ask that evening. "Nellie belongs too, it costs next to nothing."

"Out of the question," says my mother. "Even if they paid you."

"But they have songs and tracking," I insist.

"It's not for us. You can always sing songs at home. And tracking is for bloodhounds."

My father looks up.

"What are you talking about?" he asks.

"Girl Scouts," she replies.

He closes his book.

"Long before the war," he says to me, "I went camping in the islands one summer. Every time I picked up my binoculars to look at the birds, I would see the boys of the Hitler Youth. They were holding combat exercises on the beach. And who did they exercise with? With Dutch Boy Scouts! All tough guys together, very friendly. 'Unfurl the banners soaked in blood!' they would sing, in German." He pats my cheek. "And that's the kind of club you want to join?"

"It was just because of the tassels," I mumble.

"I'm not allowed to join Brownies," I tell Nellie the next day.

"Too bad," she says. "Then you're going to miss a whole lot of things, movies, tracking, things like that. And camp."

"Camp?" I repeat, wide-eyed.

Translated from the Dutch
by Arnold and Erica Pomerans

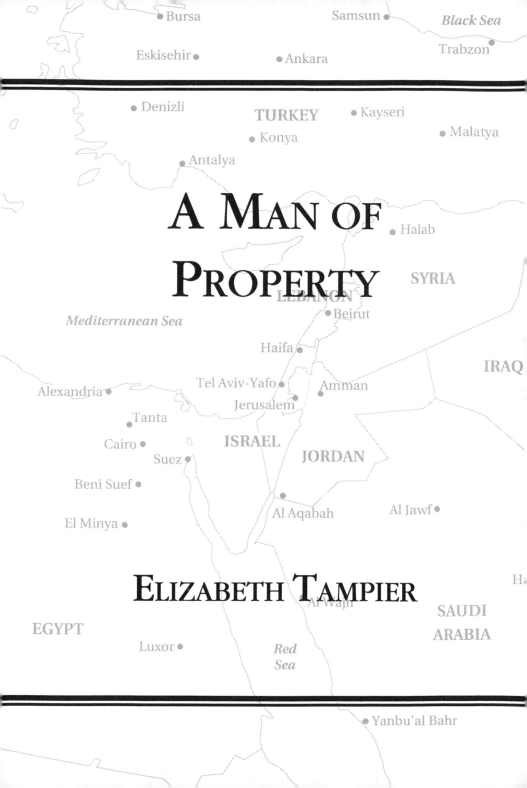

A MAN OF PROPERTY

ELIZABETH TAMPIER

Elisabeth Tampier, a French instructor and writer, was born in the United States. She has traveled extensively and has lived throughout the Arab world.

Ms. Tampier has one daughter and currently resides in Beirut, Lebanon.

Abu Fawwaz* brought us two towels to cover our legs. My skirt was long so I took the smaller one, leaving the big grayish one to Marie. The fitted skirt of Marie's city suit eased up over her knees whenever she shifted position on the carpet, showing too much leg. We shifted positions often. It wasn't too comfortable sitting on the ground.

"Welcome, welcome," said Umm Fawwaz, serving us another cup of sweet tea. "Your presence honors us."

"God's greetings on you," replied Marie, who had a degree in Arabic. She knew all the formal salutations by heart. It was part of her training as an anthropologist, I guess.

This was our mid-morning tea, and it was served with green almonds and salt. Umm Ahmed had brought them from town the night before, in the truck that brought us— Marie and her husband, me and my husband—to the *badia*** just after sunset. She'd brought fresh fruit and vegetables in great quantities. "There's nothing fresh out there except milk," she said, "so they'll be happy." The almonds were the season's first and a great delicacy, according to Marie. I wasn't crazy about them myself.

Umm Fawwaz and her husband were distant cousins of Umm Ahmed and took care of her sheep. Umm Ahmed had told us this in the truck coming out. She'd sat next to Marie and me in the back and talked about her childhood and the relatives we were going to visit.

"I used to come out here on visits with my brothers when I was little. We were so excited! You can't imagine how happy I was," she said, her face lit up suddenly by these

---

*In Arab society, parents are respectfully referred to by the name of their oldest son: Abu Fawwaz means father of Fawwaz, Umm Fawwaz means mother of Fawwaz.

**badia*—Arabic term for the semiarid steppes of the Middle East, which green with vegetation in spring and where seminomads graze their sheep.

recollections of her youth. She couldn't have been much over forty, but she talked as if this were in another century.

Her father had been a trader in *samneh*, sheep butter, and yoghurt and cheese, which he collected from nomads in the *badia* and sold to merchants in Aleppo and Raqqa. He had invested all his profits in sheep, which he then sent out to his relatives who were still nomads.

"We didn't trust the banks in those days," Umm Ahmed said with a laugh. "Maybe I'm like my father. When he died I bought sheep with my share of the inheritance. My brothers bought land or put the money in their businesses, which is proper. My sisters thought they were clever to buy gold. Then the prices went down and they lost a lot! Meat's still going up. They wish they'd been smart like me."

She laughed heartily, her plump body shaking even more than ours, jostled by the bumps and troughs in the desert track we were more or less following. The land was flat here, and the vehicles that had come before us had made several trails in the same general direction.

"Is that why you keep a sheep at home, to sell? Or are you going to eat it?" I asked. Umm Ahmed lived in a modern apartment in the newest section of Deir ez-Zor, as suited her status as the wife of a prosperous gold merchant. But the plumbing was erratic in her modern bathroom next to the master bedroom where my husband and I had been sleeping for the last week. So we too used the "family" bathroom they had added on the roof above, next to two extra bedrooms they'd built for their six children. To reach it, we had to pass a sheep tied to a post near the roof door. I knew sheep were not exactly known for their fierce temperament, but this sheep had quite a long rope. It could wander around, and it made me nervous.

Umm Ahmed stifled an incredulous look, and said: "We keep the ewe for making our own yoghurt and *samneh*. I know many of our friends and even some of my relatives buy yoghurt made out of milk powder from cows. You

find it in all the shops now. But I haven't been able to get used to the taste."

Almost as soon as we had arrived the night before we'd been served freshly made yoghurt. Umm Ahmed claimed she could tell from the taste what part of the *badia* the sheep were grazing, although I found this hard to believe. You'd think it was wine, from the fuss she made rolling it around in her mouth and the compliments she offered to our hosts.

Our husbands had disappeared shortly after dawn, when the first cup of tea was served, and I was beginning to get nervous. Was this the fourth or fifth cup that Umm Fawwaz was pouring for me now? There are no toilets in a tent, and the land all around looked depressingly flat.

"Where are the men?" I whispered to Marie when we were left alone.

"They must have gone into town for something. I saw the truck being loaded with sheep early. They move sheep from one grazing ground to another in trucks now. Our car must have been used for another errand."

I looked off into the distance. As far as the eye could see was flat land covered with a tender green veil broken by round mounds of darker green vegetation. It looked like nothing so much as a seascape on a windy day, unfathomable, impossible to navigate with anything as imprecise as the steering wheel of a car. However could they have found the way here, to this black goat tent, a mere speck in the ocean of indistinguishable steppe?

"How will they find the way back?" I asked Marie.

"Don't worry," she answered. "They might get lost once or twice. Even the bedouin don't recognize every pebble on the way. But they'll find us sooner or later."

Marie twisted her head around constantly while talking, as if alert to many things going on at the same time. Nothing seemed to escape her.

There did seem to be some sort of commotion on the other side of the big tent, closed off from the guest section by

man-high reed matting. Voices were raised, female mostly, and someone seemed to be weeping.

"What's going on, do you know?" I asked Marie. It was my first visit to eastern Syria, but she'd been coming for years.

"Umm Ahmed and Umm Fawwaz are trying to persuade Salima to return to her husband. You remember him, the good-looking fellow we saw the other night at the headman's house? He was talking about the motorcycle-cart he'd bought and what he plans to do with the extra income he'll earn from it. Khaled is a good example of the enterprising new kind of farmer. He works hard on his small plot of land, changes crops according to what sells best, and has ideas for diversifying his income. The taxi-cart is a good idea. He can carry two or three people, or a few sheep or crops to the market. It brings in a good second income in the afternoon, once his work in the fields is finished."

Marie stopped talking as the jumble of voices on the other side of the tent separated into a dialogue we could hear distinctly.

"He only wants me back so I can help weed the tomatoes and beans! And he can go back and forth to town on his fancy machine. Let his new young wife do it! I won't go back."

"Salima, my daughter Salima, listen to me." It was Umm Fawwaz speaking. "What's the good of being stubborn like this? Your children need you, your husband needs you. Are you ashamed? Did he ever beat you? Did you or your children ever go without a meal? Do you not have a roof over your head all year round and as much water as you need flowing from a tap in the courtyard? I love you, your father loves you, but your place is not with us anymore. You are not a child."

"He had no right to sell my cow. It was mine, and I could do what I liked with the income. You know that. I gave him the money I got from the cheese and milk. Nobody made me. I was so good, but did he appreciate it? I worked from

morning to night, in the house, in the fields, with the children. Am I a tired old woman that he needs a new wife? I gave him three sons and we can have more."

"Daughter, daughter, swallow your pride. Can we tell a man what to do? I understand your anger and your pain, but you must accept God's will. Of course you will have more children. Your husband will never put you aside."

"Mother, if you saw the looks she gives me when Khaled leaves the house. I am just a servant for their pleasure. How can I bear it?"

"Salima, my dear, stop your weeping." Umm Ahmed joined the talk. "Now he spoils the new wife. He is a man and he is happy. But soon you will be grateful to have help in the house and the fields, and you will show her the proper way to do things."

"Yes, my daughter," added Umm Fawwaz. "Now she is still a child. But she will learn and you will be her teacher. Be patient. Trust in God."

"But Mother, he had no right to buy her jewelry with my cow. It was my dowry, for me to keep. You made Father write it in our marriage contract. How can you forget that?"

Marie was taking notes. She always had a small notepad with her. In the evenings she and her husband and mine sat for at least an hour comparing facts they'd accumulated. This would be a rich find. It would go into their book for sure.

I was glad that I could understand, despite the difficult accent of the northeast. Women talked of simple things, using words I knew.

"I will talk to your father about the cow. But make sure in your heart it is the cow that bothers you, and not the new wife. About her we can do nothing. That you know. Now come, I must begin preparing the cheese and you can help me. It is easier than weeding, and you will feel better if your hands are busy."

Marie and I stretched our legs. One of my feet had fallen asleep and was tingling unbearably. We would soon go and

watch the cheese-making. But first I had to take a walk as far from the tent as I dared. And before the men came back, when we would be served more tea. My bladder was bursting.

The day went by slowly, very slowly. The passage of time was marked only by Abu Fawwaz' efforts to master the elements. As the sun rose higher, he tightened the cords of the tent and made small shifts in the reed-matting walls to capture the slightest passing breeze. The steppe was a sea, and by adjusting our sails to it, we remained cool and comfortable.

It was one o'clock when the men returned, with Khaled in tow. I did remember him, a tall man with a droopy mustache that gave him the air of a Mexican in an American western. With Abu Fawwaz they chased after the best lamb for our lunch. Khaled attempted to persuade his wife's father to choose a lamb from his own small stock. The guests were his friends, and he wanted to show his father-in-law he was not just anyone. He was a man of property, a man with foreign friends.

But Abu Fawwaz resisted this upstart behavior. He was the host, and hospitality was his prerogative. A wayward son-in-law must be received and treated with dignity. He, Abu Fawwaz, had chosen his daughter's husband and would not easily renounce his decision. But let him keep his place and recognize the superiority of his elders.

At least, that was Marie's interpretation, as she followed the complex negotiations involved in the reconciliation of man and wife and explained them to me.

By the time the lamb had been captured, slaughtered, cooked, and eaten, it was close to sundown.

Serious negotiations began only with digestion. Khaled kept his foreign friends close to him, the women as well as the men. We were witnesses to his respectability. He was a man of progress, he was moving ahead. On the other side of

the divided tent Umm Ahmed was huddled with Salima, her mother, and the other girls and children.

Khaled addressed his father-in-law in a steady tone. "Since I married your daughter I have increased my land three times. The work was too much for us alone, and our boys are still too small to help. My uncle's daughter is strong. She will lighten the burden for Salima."

Abu Fawwaz listened without comment. He was pleased at the delicacy his son-in-law showed in bringing up the matter of his new wife. This was the cause of his daughter's sorrow, he knew. It was no small thing for a woman to accept a second wife. Indeed, it was no longer common for a man to have more than one—unless his wife was sterile or had only daughters. He understood her anger. But Khaled was no ordinary man. He had ambitions and he achieved them. His wife would benefit too, and why should Salima disapprove of what the Prophet had permitted? A man who could support two wives was veritably a man of property.

He brought up the matter of the cow. What solution could be found for his daughter's being deprived of her rights? He was a fair man, but a contract is a contract.

"Abu Fawwaz, Uncle, with the proceeds from selling her cow I was able to buy my motor-cart. This machine has already brought in much money. It is true that I did not ask her permission, but this was a sudden opportunity. I had to decide quickly or lose the deal, and I knew the stubbornness of your daughter. Women don't always think of the future. It is we men who carry the burden of planning for our children's future.

"It is not true that I bought gold with the sale of Salima's cow. That was a wedding gift from my father. God willing, I will repay him at the end of this season, if the tomato and bean prices are as good as last year. Next year I hope to buy a pickup truck, which will bring more money than a motorcycle cart. It will also be useful for the whole family. I can help transport the sheep to the *badia* next spring, saving you money. I can bring water and the supplies you need on Fridays."

Abu Fawwaz listened without comment, but the sternness of his features relaxed. Conversation turned to the price of sheep and vegetables. Would the government keep a close control over prices and stick to the announced quotas of its purchasing offices? Marie's husband predicted that oil prices would go down. This would be good for Khaled's transportation business. Tomatoes could be grown in greenhouses when it was still cold and bring a good profit.

My husband asked for details about the contracts linking Abu Fawwaz with the owners of the sheep he took to the *badia* in the spring. Why not associate Salima to her husband's pickup business by a similar contract, to compensate her for the loss of her cow?

The idea pleased Abu Fawwaz. The support his son-in-law received from educated foreigners impressed him. They had confidence in Khaled's dynamic way of doing things. He had been right to choose him as a husband for his oldest daughter.

"Salima," he called. "Bring tea." The deal was clinched.

Salima walked next to me on the way back to the truck. Tears rolled down her face. I felt a knot in my stomach. The arm I placed briefly on her shoulder reminded me only of my awkwardness, my otherness.

"Are you sad to be going back?" I asked, not wanting to pretend I didn't see the tears flowing without interruption down her smooth brown cheeks.

"I am happy to see my children. I missed my children, and now I will see them again."

Ahead of us, I saw my husband laughing with the other men, satisfied with their mission accomplished, for they'd brought the sheep back to its fold, back to its rightful owner. A feeling of hatred surged through me as I continued to stare at my husband's receding back.

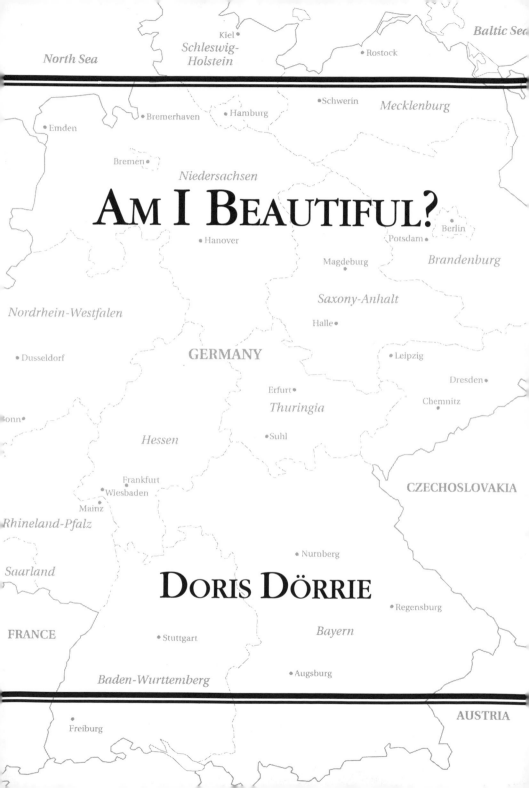

AM I BEAUTIFUL?

DORIS DÖRRIE

Doris Dörrie is a writer and filmmaker who was born in Hanover, Germany. She came to the United States in 1973 to attend the University of the Pacific in Stockton, California. Ms. Dörrie attended The New School for Social Research in New York. She later returned to Germany and enrolled in The Academy for Film and Television in Munich.

Ms. Dörrie has written and directed seven feature films and twenty-five documentaries, including *Men, Love in Germany,* and *Me and Him.* Her films have won numerous awards at film festivals around the world. She is a five-time winner of the German National Film Award for cinematography and in 1991 received the Best Mystery Movie Award. In the U.S. in 1986 she received the Charlie Chaplin Award for best comedy. Ms. Dörrie is also the author of six collections of short stories, many of which have appeared in periodicals. Two collections, *Love, Pain, and the Whole Damn Thing* and *What Do You Want from Me?,* have been published in the United States. The following selection is from her newest book, *Bin ich schön? (Am I Beautiful?).*

Ms. Dörrie resides in Munich, Germany, with her husband and daughter.

My father told my mother never to ask. But every time a woman in a bikini walks past us, I can see the words well up in my mother's mouth, trying for all their worth to get out, and the way she tries to swallow them, clenching her teeth and pressing her lips together.

Then I only have to count to ten, and there's my mother saying: Tell me the truth. Is my rear-end as fat as hers? Are my legs pitted with cellulite like that? Do I look like her? Am I prettier? Or uglier? Or just the same? I only want to know. Tell me. I won't be hurt. I swear. I just want to know where I stand.

Lucy, my father groans, please.

My mother doesn't say anything for a second. Angelina, she calls over now, come here, your shoulders are already red.

She rubs the tanning cream into my skin with quick, hard motions, until I take off, heading down to the water, passing close by all the girls in their flowery bikinis, who lie there on fluffy towels, eyes closed, a paper cup with a straw in one hand, a Walkman in the other. One girl sits up and watches me draw big circles in the sand with my toe, and a chunk of snow-white breast pops up out of her bra. She is wearing golden Bitex sunglasses that snuggle tight against her cheekbones, making her look like a dangerous insect. I'd like a pair of Bitexes myself.

I'm old, my mother says. My father sighs. Everybody promise me you'll tell me when I start to look impossible in a bikini.

My mother's body is strange. She has slender arms and legs, but a fat stomach, like a pillow that just sits there and won't really tan, with rivers of white stripes across it. It's ugly, but sometimes I'd love to touch it, it looks so soft and tender.

I hate my stomach, my mother says. No matter what I do, it won't go away. That's what having children gets you.

If she hates it so much, why doesn't she do something to get rid of it? How can she possibly run around like that, I ask myself. Why doesn't she wear a one-piece or a beach dress? Why is she determined to expose her stomach to the sun? We're on the beach every day, and every day I see her stomach.

Ah, my mother says, it's beautiful here. I don't ever want to go back.

That's the cue. I look at my father, he squinches his eyes tight. My brother Philip groans. Ben is still too small, he probably doesn't remember. Last year she didn't want to leave Italy, the year before that it was Portugal. And now it's Florida that she never wants to leave.

By afternoon she is already paging through the real-estate ads in the paper. Just for fun, she says, just curious.

That's how it always starts. Since she inherited money from my grandmother four years ago, she's had the power to change all our lives.

Bodo, she says, holding the ads under his nose, look at this. You can't even get a garage for that at home!

My father nods and doesn't say anything, the way he never says anything when it's our necks.

Just imagine what it would be like to live under palm trees! my mother bubbles enthusiastically. To wake up every morning with the sun shining! Never to have to wear panty-hose again—just think of it, Angelina!

I turn away.

Put a T-shirt on, my mother says, your back is already red. She smiles and holds my T-shirt out to me. I start to pull it on.

I can't see a thing as she whispers: Angelina—to live somewhere completely different, wouldn't that be great?

With every move I make, dried salt scours my back under the shirt. I hate that.

Girls and boys on pink mopeds buzz past along the beach road like a swarm of bees. The girls laugh with their mouths wide open, they're wearing silver and gold Bitex sunglasses. The boys grin and sneak looks at them. They're all wearing torn jeans, no shirts, their smooth tanned backs glisten like ladybug wings in the sun.

Ben is throwing sand, Philip is digging a hole fifteen feet deep, my father is staring silently out at the water, my mother lets the paper fall to one side.

Suddenly she looks as if she is going to burst into tears, but I may be wrong, because now she just gives a little sniff, lifts her chin, and claps her hands: Anybody hungry, maybe?

At the motel I stand in front of the mirror in my pale blue bikini, the top lies flat across my pigeon-egg breasts, and I'm one straight line from shoulders to feet. I'm thin, my ribs stick out like little clothes hangers, your basic ironing-board figure—but I like it. I wouldn't want to be any other way. My skin is soft and tan, like milk chocolate. I rub my flat, hard stomach. When I bend over, the thin wrinkles in the skin turn black. My legs are long and straight. I look good. I smile at myself in the mirror, my teeth glisten white in my tanned face, my eyes look bluer than usual. If I had Bitex sunglasses, I'd really be beautiful.

Angelina, my mother shouts, I could use some help!

She always makes the same thing when we're on vacation: spaghetti and salad, no matter what country we're in. She thinks we kids are crazy about spaghetti, when it's just that we're so starved after a day at the beach that we'd eat anything.

Ben is allowed to sit at the table naked and smear tomato sauce on his chest.

Isn't this great? my mother asks him for the third time now. She's really so excited and gives a silly laugh when he squirts sauce everywhere. Philip is reading a comic book under the table. My father tells him twice to put it away, but his voice sounds tired, and Philip doesn't even look up.

My parents look at each other across the table.

I'm happy, my mother says.

That's good, my father says.

You shouldn't be constantly comparing yourself to others, my mother scolds me. Even if they all have Bitex sunglasses, that doesn't necessarily mean you have to have them, too. Ask yourself which wishes truly come from your heart and which you've been talked into by advertising. Things, things, things—they don't make happiness.

From deep inside me comes the wish for Bitex sunglasses. If I had them, I'd be a different person, I know.

My mother and I drive to the supermarket, down quiet side streets, past frame houses with porches bordered by giant hibiscus with blossoms as big as saucers.

Now and then my mother drives so slow that horns honk angrily behind us. She strains to look out her window, bends way out, shielding her eyes with her hand. The third time I catch on. Every time she slows down, she has discovered a house with a sign, bigger and more colorful than those in Italy and Portugal, but with the same message: FOR SALE.

Why do you always want to live somewhere else? I ask her.

She stares at me in amazement, as if I've guessed her innermost secret. She's always thought I'm kind of dense.

Don't want to at all, she says, I just want to imagine it, is that so bad? A person can always imagine something else, damn it.

She hits the gas so hard that the car shoots away, pushing me back in my seat as if I were being shot into space.

I imagine myself a slender, grown-up woman of twenty-five, in a long dress of black chiffon by Armani or Comme des Garcons, one that flutters around my ankles with each step. I have a glass of champagne in my hand and I'm smiling. My earrings jingle with every move, my lipstick blazes bright red, I don't need anyone.

As we turn onto the highway I see a man with a cross. I saw him once before, just outside Miami, when Ben had upchucked all over the car because he was too hot. The man is tall and fat, his hair looks like a bad dye job, pineapple yellow. Across his shoulders he is carrying a gigantic wooden cross, maybe fifteen feet long, with a backpack and sleeping bag fastened to it. He is walking in the grassy median between lanes, not looking right or left, traffic thunders past him.

What a crazy, my mother says and shakes her head.

I like him. At least he's doing something different, although I have no idea why he's dragging that cross all over the place; but then what are we doing?

In the supermarket are piles of Bitexes in all colors. I put one on, they're so light you hardly notice them, the lenses are sea green, and the supermarket sinks under water. My mother gives me a green stare and shakes her head.

Oh please, I beg her, but she hardly looks at me, mutters distractedly to herself about how she mustn't forget Bodo's yogurt and that I should remind her, and shoves her cart on ahead. I stand there, watching her go, as if saying good-bye, I could just lose myself right here and now and make it on my own. Alone in America.

Ten years later I'd call home and the spinach green telephone in the hall would ring. My mother shouts angrily from the kitchen: Why doesn't somebody get that? She comes down the hall, her hands still wet, and just as she reaches for the phone, it stops ringing.

She shoves the cart intentionally against my butt. Angelina, she nags, don't just stand there like a dummy, I could use some help.

Next to the supermarket she discovers a shoe store. She gazes dreamily at a pair of dark blue high-heeled sandals.

Just to look, she says.

She minces back and forth in front of the mirror in the shoes, thrusting her breasts out. I notice her belly bulging

55

under her thin dress. She rips open a box and pushes a pair of red sandals into my hand. Try these on, she says, aren't they cute?

I shake my head.

And when I *do* try to give you something, she says, you just make a face. She angrily packs the sandals back in their box, runs barefoot around the shop, and tries on a pair of garish yellow stilettos. She has really pretty legs, just like mine. They're younger than her face. She laughs and admires herself in the shoes, she prances back and forth, and in the mirror I see the woman that I otherwise know only from old photographs. In those she's young, her skin as taut as that of the girls on the beach, she is wearing a close-fitting flowered dress and holding a fat baby on one arm, me. When you were little, she sometimes says to me, you hugged me and kissed me and told me how much you loved me.

I cannot remember the two people she is talking about. I find it annoying and a little embarrassing when she talks like that, it makes me feel like someone who's been dropped on her head and has forgotten everything.

How do you like the shoes? she asks, turning around to me.

Sexy, I say, because I can see how much she likes them.

Really? she says and grins. I nod.

She comes over to me, whispers: You don't think I look silly in these shoes? Old biddy dolled up like a chick? She smiles, unsure of herself. I would like to hug her and kiss her and tell her how much I love her. I shrug and look away. There is a pause.

Ah well, she says, why bother. She takes the shoes off and puts them back neatly, slips into her old sandals, and leaves the store without a glance my way.

She has an appointment to see a house the next day. Just for fun, she says, just curious. It doesn't obligate us to anything.

My father doesn't say a word.

Good God, she says, stamping her foot, I simply would like to see one of these houses on the inside, that's all!

Where would we go to school? Philip asks.

She glares at him. You'll be the death of me, she screams, you'll be the death of me yet!

She vanishes into the kitchen and rattles dishes as she washes up.

What's wrong with her? Philip asks. I shrug. My father turns on the TV.

A fat black woman in a mustard yellow suit is holding a microphone under teenage noses.

What are they talking about? I ask my father.

She's asking them, if they had the choice, whether they would rather be attractive or intelligent, he translates. Which would you choose?

Attractive, Ben and I say, both at once.

My father sighs and turns the TV off again. Lucy, he calls, if you had the choice, would you rather be attractive or intelligent?

She comes out of the kitchen, a sieve on her head, a strand of spaghetti draped over each ear, her forefinger in her mouth. I think I'd like to be intelligent, she says, I'm already attractive.

The real estate agent is young and cool. He has very black, longish hair and wears blue-metallic Bitexes with silver lenses. His Nike shoes have been left untied, which makes a big impression on Philip—as he sees it, only really megacool guys leave their Nikes untied.

Are you Mrs. Winter? the agent asks my mother.

She is wearing her best dress and lipstick. The collar is rumpled, so that the label is visible. Yes, she warbles in English, and this is my family. I can't stand it when she speaks English.

He shakes hands firmly with us all. My hand is sweaty, his

noticeably cool in the heat. His name is Douglas. My
mother introduces us all, even Ben, who is perched on my
father's shoulders. Angelina—Douglas repeats my name
as if he were sucking on candy.

He unlocks the house and goes in ahead of us. It is dark
and smells like cat piss and wet dogs. There are antiques
everywhere. Pictures of dead rabbits and gloomy forests
hang on all the walls. The bed in the bedroom is covered
with green silk. Photos of two men, both with mustaches
and holding cats and dogs in their arms, are stuck into the
bathroom mirror. Dozens of shiny earrings hang from a
piece of barbed wire. My mother leaves at once, my father
doesn't even bother to look at the bathroom.

For a moment I am alone, I wonder if I should pocket a
pair of earrings shaped like bunches of grapes, but I could
never wear them. My mother would cross-examine me
like the cops till I told her where I got them.

Douglas leads us out into the yard. Three dogs, two big
and one very tiny, are sitting on an old, tattered couch
watching television. They barely turn their heads, the little
one lets out a quick yelp. It's a commercial for tampons.
There are dog turds all around the swimming pool.

Douglas apologizes lamely. My mother doesn't look at
any of us. She inspects everything with a smile and nods.

Yes well, she says at last, I think we've seen enough,
haven't we? She turns to my father. He nods in silence.

In the entry, just inside the front door, is a folding screen.
Philip looks behind it and does not come out again, until I
look back there, too, and find him sitting in a black leather
swing, grinning. Above him are two leather rings dan-
gling from iron chains. Now everyone looks behind the
screen.

Hmm, Douglas says.

To each his own, my father says in German.

Philip, come out from behind there at once, my mother
says.

We stand around in front of the house, not saying anything. Philip kicks a tire on our rental. My father shows Ben a bee sucking on a hibiscus blossom.

It's a house you could really do something with, Douglas says.

Certainly, my mother says, but it's not exactly what we had in mind. My father casts her a sidelong glance.

Tell me about what you do have in mind, Douglas says, and plays with his Bitexes. Ben grabs them.

Don't, my mother says.

Oh, Douglas says, let him do what he wants, these are unbreakable glasses. He grins. We can be frank here: It's an awful house. My company insists I always show it first, for shock effect, so to speak, so that afterward all the others look neat and tidy.

My mother giggles. Oh, I see, she says.

I would love to rip those Bitexes out of Ben's hands, put them on, take off.

The neighbors at the next house, Douglas says, are especially quiet. It's beside a cemetery.

My mother beams at him. My father takes the glasses away from Ben and gives them back to Douglas. Ben wails.

Could I ride in your car with you? Douglas asks.

Why, of course, my mother cries. My father's eyebrows go up.

Douglas sits beside me, I can smell his lemony after-shave.

He drums his fingers on the armrest. Angelina, he says, what a pretty name.

I don't reply, I don't like to speak English. The words just won't fit in my mouth, and I hate making mistakes. His thigh presses lightly against mine. Intentionally, or because he can't help it in the narrow back seat? I take a deep breath and pull my leg away a fraction of an inch. Nothing happens for a while, then Douglas bends forward and his knee is pressed hard against mine.

Are you looking purely for a vacation home or do you intend to spend more time in Florida? he asks my parents.

My mother opens her mouth. Actually, we're hoping to move here, she says. Europe is getting to be a weird place. War and depression everywhere, you know what I mean?

The car turns quiet. My father casts my mother a sidelong glance.

She stretches and smiles in the rear-view mirror.

I do, Douglas says, and falls back again in the seat, his upper arm pressing against mine.

Sorry, he says, pulling his arm away again and putting on his Bitexes.

We look at seven more houses. In one of them framed baby clothes hang on the wall, in another there is a huge empty cage in an impeccably tidy bedroom. You can see the vacuum-cleaner tracks in the carpet around the cage.

What do you think, Bodo? my mother asks in each house. My father shrugs and offers a patient smile.

I'm thirsty, Philip whines.

We're only looking at five houses tomorrow, Douglas tells him.

Philip groans, I hold my breath. Tomorrow? my father says.

My mother smiles and scans us all. Till tomorrow, she says to Douglas.

He makes the hint of a bow. *Ciao*, Angelina, he says to me.

Just picture it, my mother says, you could go to the beach after school, on weekends we could rent a boat and have picnics out in the ocean. We'd all have deep tans and always look healthy, and never have colds. We'd all like ourselves better.

We have to tell Douglas that we're not serious about this, my father says.

Tomorrow, my mother says, we'll tell him tomorrow.

In the first house we look at the next day, an old woman with smeared lipstick and still in her nightgown is sitting watching TV. It's a nature program. I sit down beside her, my father puts Ben on my lap. Ben stretches a hand out to the old woman, and she takes it in her own trembling hand. Dogs are running across the screen. Bow-wow, the old woman says to Ben, and Ben gives her an indulgent look.

Her children want to sell the house, Douglas says to my mother in a low voice, they're in a hurry, so the price is good.

But my mother doesn't like the way it's laid out. Besides, the house doesn't have a porch.

The old woman gives Ben a good-bye kiss on the head. Ben starts wailing.

Douglas has already reached to open the door on Philip's side of the car, but thinks better of it, walks clear around the car, and opens the door on my side. He doesn't look at me as he gets in.

What's worse, Philip says, licking a man's hairy leg or swallowing a cow's eye?

Bag it, I say.

What's worse, he says, drinking armpit sweat or foot sweat?

Philip! my mother shouts from the driver's seat.

What's worse, he whispers, slipping on dog crap or kissing a real-estate agent?

My mother is lying on a lounge chair on the beach, paging through catalogs. They are illustrated with houses, tiny as toys, one beside the other. My father squats beside her in the sand, he'll pay for only one lounge chair a day, they're damned expensive, he says.

I can only vaguely hear my parents' conversation above the music from my Walkman. The batteries are running low, the music starts to fade in and out. I turn the Walkman off, but don't take off the earphones.

I'd love a palm tree in front of my house, a big palm tree, my mother says.

How long are you going to keep this game up? my father asks.

One more day, she says.

I don't understand, he says, why do you get yourself caught up in dreams that will never come true?

Why shouldn't I? she says, Explain it to me.

Just how do you imagine it all?

If we wanted to, we could live a totally different life, she says and rests her hands on her stomach.

My father turns away and pokes at the sand with a stick. I can't make you happy, he says, stands up, and walks down to the water. His thighs and back are dusted with sand, from the rear he looks like a breaded cutlet.

My mother looks all around, seems confused, as if she's lost her way.

Angelina, she bellows, since she thinks I can't hear her, put some lotion on your shoulders!

I'm sitting in the swing on the porch, all the others are in the house. It's an old house, the paint is flaking off the wood shingles, cockroaches as big as frogs skitter across the floor. There are wide cracks in the cement floor of the porch, with grass growing in them.

Douglas sits down beside me on the swing. The scent of lemon sloshes over me like a wave.

I lay my head way back, because I don't know where else to look. There are branches of a deep-purple bougainvillea over our heads.

My mother comes out the door.

I think I'm about to fall in love, she says, did you see the room on the second floor? She vanishes into the house again.

Douglas balances his Bitexes on his thigh. I pick them up and put them on. Six o'clock, the Exxon station, he says in a low voice.

I look at him through his Bitexes, his skin is a shimmery blue, as if it were cold. I'm feeling confident, adult, beautiful.

He lifts his sunglasses from my nose. I'm coming, Mrs. Winter, he calls. As if attached to a rubber band, I reluctantly follow him.

A young girl with straw-blond hair is sitting at a sewing machine in the living room. A dog, blond like her and with blue eyes, is lying at her feet.

It's a good house, she says to my mother, it's got good vibes. People with evil in their hearts don't last long here. We had a guy here once who put little labels on all his stuff in the fridge. He only stayed a week. When he left, he stole my watch. She sighs, scratches her dog behind its ears, and goes back to rattling away at her sewing machine.

You can see the ocean from the room on the second floor. Douglas climbs out through the window onto the roof and gives my mother, then me, his hand. He squeezes my hand gently before letting go again.

The tar-board roof smolders under my feet. Two tall palm trees clatter in the wind. My father is standing down below in front of the porch. At his feet Ben is playing with fallen bougainvillea blossoms. The blond girl comes out of the house and unlocks her bike. She puts Ben up on the seat and pushes him around in a circle. My father stands in the middle of the circle, the pale dog runs along behind the bike. From up here they look like a perfect little family. They love each other and eat corn flakes for breakfast in a room flooded with light, they run laughing across springtime meadows, their shiny hair floating in the wind, they snuggle up in front of the fireplace, in snow-white bathrobes and with thick socks on their feet.

My mother lifts her hand to wave at them, and then lets it fall again. Just imagine it, she says to me.

Douglas looks at me and licks his lips.

He is leaning against the gas pump for super lead-free; from a distance he looks arrogant, in a bad mood. His arms are crossed, his eyes hidden behind his Bitexes. He doesn't see me. I'm standing behind a billboard advertising trips to Mexico. The tepid wind brushes over my legs, dives under my dress, and billows the fabric till I look pregnant. I have clean panties on, my stomach is cramping as if I've eaten something that's turned bad.

I have to be back home before it gets dark, in forty-five minutes.

I see every minute until then lying before me like the steps up the Mayan ruins on the billboard. They lead straight up to nothing, to an empty, cold sky. There is no reason to climb them. You can see from below what you expect up top.

I don't even like Douglas.

Once I realize that I don't even like him especially, my stomach calms down. I am stronger than Douglas. I make my move.

Hi, I say.

We drive to a lonely spot in the mangrove swamps, brown water stagnating in ponds to the right and left of the road, in the distance the shimmering turquoise of the sea. Pelicans fly overhead.

I watch their flight while he touches me. They suddenly plunge as if they'd been shot, hit the water beak-first, disappear, and come up again, take a quick swallow—you can tell from the jerk in their throat—look around as if they've eaten the icing off the cake at a fancy party, drift for a moment on the waves, and then like some tired old airplane they take off again, and the whole thing starts all over.

His hand slips lower, plays now with the elastic of my panties, snapping it against my skin, and then the hand abruptly dives.

Quick as lightning, I grab it tight, as if I were catching a fish with my hand.

Please, he whispers in my ear, please. You are so beautiful. You are driving me crazy.

Forty-eight dollars, I say.

The sun out there drops like an orange into the sea; it's ice-cold in the car, the air-conditioning is on, I can see the goose bumps on my stomach. He lays the green money on the dashboard, he laughs. How much for your heart? he says.

I furtively pay for the glasses at the checkout while my mother is getting milk and yogurt. I tuck them under my shirt. The glasses touch my breasts, which now know one more person than they did just yesterday.

When my mother doesn't return, I saunter back to the dairy department down rows of corn flakes and crackers.

She is propping herself with one arm against the dairy case full of yogurt. Her head is hanging, her breath makes little clouds in the cold of the giant refrigerator, little red rivulets trickle down her legs.

Mama, I say and feel as helpless as if I were three years old. Mama.

She stands up straight, beads of sweat on her forehead, her face as white as wax. She grimaces. Damn, she says, can't depend on anything anymore. She dabs her legs with a handerkerchief, then grabs a plastic container of milk from the case, heaves it into her cart, and pushes it to the checkout as if nothing has happened.

My father doesn't come to the beach with us, he's going to stay in bed and read the paper. Philip gives him a good-bye punch to the ribs.

My father looks up briefly. Lucy? he says, but my mother is already out the door with Ben—plus sand bucket, shovel, suntan lotion, and towels. I follow her with Philip.

She doesn't change at the beach, but sits in her dress cross-legged on the sand and silently digs a hole for Ben.

Aren't we going to look at houses today? I ask.

She shakes her head. I stand next to her, my shadow falls across her lap. My throat swells up from all the long complicated things I want to say to her. Mama, I begin.

She sticks out a hand. Look at that, she says, it's the man with the cross!

He is dragging his cross through the sand, close to the water, past all the pretty girls in their flowery bikinis, past young men in bermudas and Bitexes. He props his cross against a boulder and begins passing out little cards.

He finally comes over to us, too. My mother holds out her hand. The picture on the card is of him with his cross, underneath is printed: "Why?"

Explain it to me, my mother says and gazes earnestly at him.

He comes a step closer, squats down in front of her. He runs his hand through his pineapple yellow hair and smiles shyly.

I was a jerk, he says, an alcoholic and a jerk. Until Jesus called me. He gave me a job to do. I've already walked six thousand miles for Him. I've had five crosses stolen already. I don't own a thing, but He takes care of me. Each day brings what it brings. He falls silent.

I admire you, my mother says.

He smiles. I'm just doing my job, he says. God bless you, ma'am. He stands up and walks on.

My mother watches him go, then turns her head to give me a quick look and says apropos of nothing: When you were two, we took our vacation at the shore in Spain. I went for a swim and you stood there on the beach in your red swimsuit, screaming, you didn't want me to leave you. I wasn't allowed to take a step without you. Sometimes all I had to do was move just a little, and you'd start screaming. You did it longer than other kids, and I didn't know why. I would never have left you alone, never. For two years I carried you around with me, because I read a book that claimed babies who are constantly carried around, the way native Indian or African women do it, turn out more confident and less afraid than other children.

I kept on swimming farther, and everything was so peaceful out there, the moon was already in the sky, although it was only early afternoon, I was alone, all alone for the first time since you were born. It was so quiet and beautiful out there that I kept on swimming, farther and farther, as if I had to. Until my fingernails turned dark blue and I began to shake from the exertion. I never wanted to come back.— And you knew that. When I came out of the water I heard you crying, and Bodo said he simply couldn't get you to stop. Everybody on the beach stared at me, blaming me.

She pauses and brushes the sand from Ben's face.

You always knew that about me, she says. But it has nothing to do with any of you, do you understand?

I cram one hand into my backpack and clasp my Bitexes tight. Yes, I say, I understand.

A fat-assed woman in a silver bikini walks past us.

Angelina, my mother says, tell me the truth, is my rear-end as fat as hers?

During the night, when they are all asleep, I put on my glasses in the dark. I smile, and the edges of the lenses scrape lightly against my cheeks. I can hear Ben's rapid baby breathing, my father's snores, Philip's restless tossing in his sleep. The only one I don't hear is my mother. She sleeps without making a sound.

I lay my head back into the pillow, the night is golden black. I close my eyes behind my sunglasses, and I know that I will never be the same again.

Translated from the German
by John E. Woods

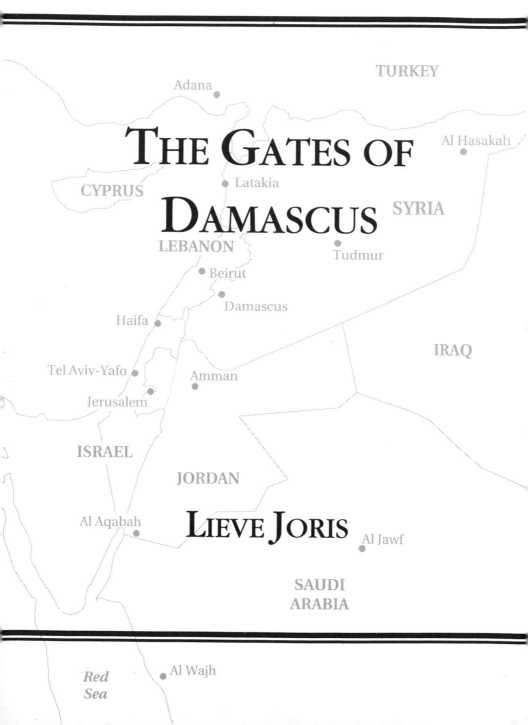

THE GATES OF
DAMASCUS

CYPRUS

TURKEY

Adana

Al Hasakah

Latakia

SYRIA

LEBANON

Tudmur

Beirut

Damascus

Haifa

IRAQ

Tel Aviv-Yafo

Amman

Jerusalem

ISRAEL

JORDAN

LIEVE JORIS

Al Aqabah

Al Jawf

SAUDI
ARABIA

Kayseri

Erzurum

Red
Sea

Al Wajh

Lieve Joris was born in Neerpelt, Belgium. After attending the School for Journalism, she was for many years the editor of the weekly *Haagse Post*. Ms. Joris has traveled extensively in the Congo, Hungary, Trinidad, Zaire, and the Middle East.

Ms. Joris has written several books documenting her travels, including *Back to the Congo* and *De melancholieke revolutie* (The Melancholy Revolution), for which she was awarded the Henriette Roland Holst Prize in 1992.

The following selection is an excerpt from Ms. Joris' most recent book, *De poorten van Damascus* (The Gates of Damascus).

Hala has put on weight and bleaches her hair like many of the local women, but her way of looking at things is refreshingly familiar. She nudges me and with a meaningful nod points out the mustachioed conductor of the military band in the park—he's practically swimming in his jacket with its heavy epaulets. What pompous gestures! And the musicians, involved with their instruments, don't pay him the slightest attention.

"Why aren't there any violins, Mama?"

Hala runs her hand through Asma's hair. "Because it's marching music. Can you imagine marching to war with violins? You need trumpets at least!"

This is our first walk through Damascus, and I feel almost blind at her side; she leads me to familiar places, and slowly the memories come back. Above the entrance to the *suq*, the bazaar, hangs a panoramic painting of a laughing Hafez Al-Assad, with Damascus as a miniature city in the background. The president glances out of the corner of his eye, which gives him a shifty look—not a very flattering image. The city is filled with such pictures. Young, old, wearing glasses and without, since my arrival he has appeared to me in many forms. This morning I even saw a Mercedes tear by with his image on its visors.

"I don't remember his being so ubiquitous."

"He brought the idea back from North Korea," Hala says with a knowing smile. "Since his visit there he's had the whole country pasted up. As if we didn't know what he looks like!"

Near the Umayyad mosque part of the *suq* has been torn down, ostensibly so the president can be driven here to pray on holy days, but everyone knows the real reason: If there is an uprising in Damascus, tanks must be able to reach the old city.

Hala drags me down to the spice bazaar with its aroma of coffee, cinnamon, and nutmeg. Light falls through holes in the corrugated iron roof mottling the cobblestones. We pause in front of a small shop selling herbs and medicinal remedies; on one of the wooden shelves is a glass bowl of dried sea horses. In English, the shopkeeper has labeled it: *Animal from the sea to make the man strong at night in the bed.*

We laugh and wander further through the narrow streets of the old city. Hala looks at the death announcements pasted to lampposts and walls and studies the photos of the deceased, figuring out how old they were. She says it is a strange quirk of hers, something she did even as a child.

Excited voices waft into the street from open windows. Asma pricks up her ears. "It's her favorite radio program," Hala whispers. Every week they broadcast a dramatization of a famous murder.

"What is it about this time?"

Hala listens. It concerns a case that caused quite a stir about ten years ago. A female student was murdered at the University of Damascus. To quell the panic that broke out, a young man was arrested at random and hanged. "It's difficult to uncover the truth about a crime in this country," she sighs. Many years ago, a town in the north of the country was in an uproar after a series of young girls were raped. The man they arrested confessed to fifteen of the rapes, but most of the girls were ashamed to admit what had happened. It was a closed city—the parents of a raped girl may murder her because she is no longer a virgin. No one dared to write about this incident out of fear of stirring up unrest.

We have walked on as we talked, but now Asma tugs impatiently on Hala's arm. "Where are we going, Mama?"

"Noplace special, we're just taking a walk."

"But where to?" Asma doesn't understand. It is the middle of summer, the sun is beating down on us mercilessly, she wants to go home. When we finally consent, she does a little dance of delight.

They live in a neighborhood where the streets have no names, the houses no numbers. Their house is separated from the street by a wall, but the woman on the third floor across the street can look right into the front room. She sits at the window all day, a white scarf around her head. When she's not there, her son takes over. They see who goes down the street, who enters the grocery store, when someone leaves their house, who comes home when. They see Asma playing soccer with her friends and later pounding on the iron gate, a bag of *bizr*, salted sunflower seeds, in her hand.

I fail to understand why we don't sit in the courtyard, in the pleasant shade of the fig tree. Until one afternoon when I hang up the laundry. The neighbors in the back stare out of their window too. They don't even move from the window when I stare back.

Hala had written to me about this house. That it was larger than the previous one, that there was enough room for me to come. I had imagined it differently, and I felt somewhat disappointed as I lugged my bags over the threshold. A narrow hallway, a sitting room with a checkered sofa, a bedroom, a small kitchen with a granite counter. High atop the wardrobe in the bedroom a plastic flower arrangement, wrapped in cellophane. The large Shanghai clock in the hall had stopped.

But Hala, I soon realize, is happy here. She has always dreamed of having three things: a bathroom, a telephone, and a washing machine. She had to fight hard, but she has all three. If she moved now, she would have to pay ten times as much for such a house.

Later I notice how carefully she has laid out the rooms. The blue of the sofa complements the flowered curtains, and everywhere I find traces of her fight against the lack of space. The wedding presents that were kept under her bed in the old house now sit on top of the wardrobe. The folding table in the hall travels throughout the house, from the little kitchen, where we eat lunch, to the front room, where we eat when the TV is on. It is Hala's writing-table, Asma's play-and-homework table.

The moment we are inside Hala flings her clothes on the bed and disappears into the bathroom. The bare room with a boiler, tap, and plastic basin turns into a Turkish bath full of steam and foam. Sitting on a low stool she lathers her skin and then pours water over herself. She washes off the heat of our walk, the dust of the streets. Wrapped in a bath towel she comes out laughing, content, the steam rolling out behind her like a cloud. "On the first day God created the earth," she says, "on the second day He created the bath." She slips into a nightgown, a habit that surprises me at first but which I will soon adopt myself.

Asma is lying on the sofa in the front room watching cartoons, the bag of *bizr* on her lap. On the large bed in the bedroom, we listen to the latest tape by the Lebanese singer Fayruz. Now and then a fig falls from the tree in the courtyard with a soft plop, the cry of a neighbor's child can be heard.

Forty years ago this neighborhood lay at the outskirts of Damascus, but since then it has curled up comfortably against the city. In reality it's a village, although the residents come from all over and have little in common. Last year a propane tank exploded in a house a few blocks away. It happened in the middle of the night, women ran outside in their housecoats. Five dead. The house has since been repaired, but no one walks by without thinking about that night. Through such calamities the neighborhood accrues a history in spite of itself. That afternoon Hala tells me about another incident that the neighbors will not easily forget.

Hala was in an advanced stage of pregnancy when she and her husband moved here. Her aunt, a former nurse, offered to help her with the delivery, but the birth was so difficult that Hala was afraid she wouldn't make it. Halfway through, her aunt gasped: "Shall I call the hospital? Wouldn't you rather go there?" As though that were still possible! Her sister Zahra pushed against her legs clumsily —the soreness would last for days.

Hala had asked Ahmed to stay at her side, but he found it such a gruesome spectacle that he fled to the front room and finally even left the house. It was an uneasy period in their relationship. That was Ahmed for you, always brimming over with revolutionary ideas but at a complete loss when it came to a little infant. He wanted to have her sleep between them at night. Such a small body, such tiny fingers, Hala was afraid he would crush her in his sleep.

When Asma was only a week old he wanted to take her with him to the market. She's still much too little for that, Hala protested, but he wrapped Asma in a blanket and left. He brought her back an hour later: It was no fun, he complained, the baby hadn't even looked around, she slept the whole time!

But there were other moments as well. Hala had heard that if you placed a newborn in the water it could swim right away. Maybe they should try it. It was an exciting idea. They placed a tub of water under the fig tree and let Asma glide down into it. It was touching to see the little tyke flounder in the tub, but if they hadn't pulled her out she would surely have drowned.

Asma was one month old when the doorbell rang one afternoon. Hala had not yet recovered from the delivery, she was feverish and fatigued. She had just prepared a pan of mutton shanks, Ahmed's favorite dish. She opened the gate and stood facing a crowd of men with rifles at the ready. "Where's your husband?" They pushed her aside and stormed in. There were at least thirty men. The whole house was full of them, and they began turning the place upside down. Hala moved frantically from room to room. What were they looking for? "We're not Muslim

Brothers*," she said. She knew that the *mukhabarat*, the Syrian security police, had been rounding them up for a few weeks now.

"That's not why we're here," the men snarled at her. "You people are Marxists." They jammed all the papers, letters, and newspapers they could find into bags, then most of them left. Six agents stayed behind. They would wait for Ahmed, they announced grimly.

The smell of mutton shanks filled the house. Ahmed might come home any minute. How could she warn him? She only hoped he had heard something. Or that he would notice the unusual commotion on the street, where agents were bustling about with their walkie-talkies.

The baby began to cry. Hala picked her up, tried to soothe her, and then started crying herself. The doorbell rang. It was a friend of Ahmed's. She caught a glimpse of his bewildered face, before they grabbed him and led him away. Everyone who rang the bell that day was arrested.

But Ahmed didn't show up. When the agents made preparations to spend the night in the front room, she retreated to the bedroom. She had cried for hours and now her cheeks were burning with fever. In the semidarkness she saw the checkered pajamas that Ahmed had carelessly thrown over the bars of Asma's crib that morning. The door opened, someone crept into the room. He went to the crib and picked up the pajamas. Her heart pounded wildly: Ahmed had come! "You must go!" she whispered. "The house is full of *mukhabarat*, they're looking for you!"

But when she awoke she was alone in bed and the house was filled with the crackling of walkie-talkies and men's voices. Ahmed had been caught the day before as he turned onto the street. Later she would learn that he had been

*Muslim Brothers—political group in several Arab countries calling for an Islamic political and social system and opposed to Western political and cultural influence.

horribly tortured that first night—and while he was being tortured his spirit had come to her in a feverish dream.

The men stayed. They were apparently expecting more visitors. The first to come was her mother. The neighbors had called to tell her something strange was going on in Hala's house. The agents forced her to stay. She slept on a bench in the courtyard, cooked for the *mukhabarat*, and sent them out on shopping errands. Asma cried every night and spit out her pacifier repeatedly.

One evening a drunken friend came to call. When he came face to face with the *mukhabarat*, he began shrieking; he tore his shirt and shouted that he was one of them. They dragged him inside and called their chief. As it turned out, he did work for the *mukhabarat*; which did not stop them, however, from arresting him.

Gradually things quieted down. Hala suspected that the roundup had spread throughout the entire city. In the meantime everyone had probably gone into hiding or been arrested. It turned out that the agents were waiting for one of the key players in the Communist splinter group to which Ahmed belonged, but he never arrived. After fourteen days they withdrew.

Translated from the Dutch
by Sam Garrett

SHAME

SUSAN HOLAHAN

Susan Holahan holds a PhD in English and a law degree from Yale University. She has taught at the University of Rochester and Yale University.

A free-lance writer, Ms. Holahan has worked as a features editor, restaurant reviewer, book reviewer, and columnist for a number of newspapers and journals, including *Newsday* and *The Advocate* of Stamford, Connecticut. In 1989, she was awarded a scholarship to the Bread Loaf Writers Conference. Her short stories and poetry have appeared in several publications, including *American Short Fiction*, *Agni*, and *Black Warrior Review*.

Ms. Holahan, who grew up in Long Island, New York, lives in Rochester with her husband, the novelist Thomas Gavin.

If you remember President Roosevelt died in nursery school, you remember the day grown-ups cried for the first time. Ellen Malkoff remembers their tears, her awe. She tends to forget that that day was also her fifth birthday. Her funny aunt got off the bus at the top of the street in tears. After dinner the birthday girl, fuddled by pot roast and adult emotion, blew out all the candles on the cake at once and waited for applause. Her mother looked at her aunt—and they both began sobbing again. Any ordinary day of the week it was wartime. You had to let the radio talk.

By junior high the war had turned cold, but adults still had the world on their minds. Ellen Malkoff would promise herself romantic attention from someone interesting on her own level. Someone like Michael Gordon—who had become *the* cute boy in class when the sixth grades from two schools mixed in the new Great Neck Junior High. Dark curly hair, dark eyes. Calling him cute simply gave you someone to say you were thinking about. Michael Gordon was no talker, so you didn't have to get to know him. You didn't have to worry if he liked you. *Someone* had to be cute. He could last for years. But Michael Gordon didn't talk. Who knew what he noticed?

Disgusting Don Seitzman, *the* loud asker of hard questions, had the tan hair of a know-it-all. You heard his hard voice everywhere. For example, he dreamed up a weird, Don-Seitzman way to let everyone in Social Studies know that *he* knew that the new teacher, Mr. LeVine, was Jewish. "You wouldn't think I'd be a *Leave-eye* with my name, Seitzman, and he'd be a *Co-hane* with the name LeVine, would you?" When Don Seitzman blatted out this question that you could tell no one was supposed to answer anyway, Ellen Malkoff for one puzzled so furiously over

how the hell sloppymouth Don Seitzman knew about
Leave-eyes and Co-hanes—was it a bar-mitzvah thing?—
that she hardly wondered at Mr. LeVine, blushing and
mumbling at the front of the room. Public Jewishness for a
teacher was different from universal Jewishness among
students. This she could accept as another fierce but
unspoken Rule for Life. Her private rule: Avoid Don
Seitzman's attention. *Not* romantic.

On exactly Ralph Zelber's actual thirteenth birthday IKE
became president. Ellen Malkoff was among those teasing
Ralph: Now he could roll his sleeves up. With those plaid
sleeves flapping on his skinny arms he didn't seem to care
what he looked like. Her, with her messy dark hair and
glasses—always talking too much or not paying attention
at all. Who was her best friend, after all? Ralph Zelber and
Don Seitzman were known friends. They probably invited
each other to their bar mitzvahs, and no girls or Michael
Gordon. About six weeks after Ralph Zelber's birthday,
the radio news that went with breakfast said Joseph Stalin
had died. Carrying the news of Stalin's death into school
felt dirty like knowing you had a Kotex pad strapped to
an elastic belt inside your underpants. Thinking about
Stalin too much had left friends of the Malkoffs without
teaching jobs, too poor to reupholster their sofa. Of course
Don Seitzman said it out loud in Social Studies. "Mr.
LeVine, you know Joe Stalin died this morning, don't
you?" Mr. LeVine blushed. Michael Gordon's face looked
so blank at the mention of Stalin that Ellen Malkoff
couldn't count any of this knowledge as romantic.

A Sunday night in April, a roar in her right ear broke up
the dead black middle of the night. This trouble was *inside*
her own ear. The Holland Tunnel was stuck in her right
ear with the lights off. You couldn't see the shine of the
tiles; you just heard the roar of the traffic. After the mid-
dle-of-the-night doctor, she dozed through days of antibi-
otics, but when someone got ready to pour hydrogen

peroxide into the ear she sat up and screamed. In the grip of total recall of the endless raw sting of hydrogen peroxide on her knee when she'd ripped open the kneecap on moss-covered rocks in a stream in the country, she screamed. Knees are thick. Knees are used to it. But "My ear! This is my *ear*. It's going to hurt. I don't think I can stand it. You can't do that to me!" Holding her down hard, they poured hydrogen peroxide, raw, from the bottle into the upside ear. Deep inside the ear, the vicious hydrogen peroxide felt benign as ginger ale, just loud. Bubbles bounced noisily off tunnel walls. Bubbles, but no sting.

This Ellen Malkoff felt like a mysterious stranger the Monday she finally went back to school. When she saw Michael Gordon in the hall by the homeroom lockers, he didn't say anything—too dazzled by her strangeness to express his admiration. She walked into Social Studies hugging books against breasts that stuck out too much for comfort when she tucked her red sweater into her skirt and pulled a wide belt tight. She slid into her seat in the second row of wood-and-metal cages with wide right arms for writing. "What happened to *you*?" Don Seitzman yelled across bare gray linoleum that stretched from one arm of the U of desks to the other. As that voice made her desperate to disappear, she grasped the permanent potential disaster in this business of romantic: Put yourself out there and you have no say in what comes back.

"What *happened* to you?" Don Seitzman yelled again while she piled books on the writing arm. In a big bright red sweater and a black-and-white wool skirt with several stiff petticoats under it, you couldn't shrink far. But Don Seitzman. Counting her books, she considered inventing a family trip that mysteriously took her away for weeks. She could not discuss her ear across four yards of gray-and-brown linoleum with twenty people including Michael Gordon listening. She reached down for the shoulder bag that had slid off onto the floor. She looked up, finally, to see Mr. LeVine waiting to start class. At the end of class Don Seitzman scooted across open floor. With his voice way out in front of him he chased Ellen Malkoff down the row of seats to the door. He wanted to know something. She ran from the classroom, her shoulder bag slamming her knee as she hurried down the hall.

June, then, the Friday before school was out, Ellen Malkoff stayed awake all night, terrified. The "atom spies" trial didn't look good for the Jews, the protests looked even worse for the Jews, the endless appeals did the Jews no good at all. A man and a woman who could look like your own parents if you looked at the photographs side-ways—not possible they could get officially killed, in public, in America. Jews prosecuting, Jews judging, a Jewish mother with children to leave alone? In an electric chair? The electric chair involved the Last Dinner *murderers* asked for in pieces of the *New York Post* left around the house after people read the columns: steak if they were skinny, spaghetti if they were fat. Ellen Malkoff trembled, awake in her dark room as though They would stay alive while her eyes stayed open.

She had been thirteen for months already. She knew you didn't mention death or sex in your own house, whatever was in the newspaper, so Saturday she couldn't tell whether she had kept Them alive. Sunday was dead time. No one walked into school sleepless on Monday. No one said a word about what must have happened Friday, sometime; because the air felt—dead. Michael Gordon never said a word anyway, of course, but even Don Seitzman didn't say *Rosenberg, Ethel and Julius Rosenberg*, in Social Studies.

That fall, when Sandie Berg invited the whole class to her late thirteenth birthday party, Ellen Malkoff looked forward to Michael Gordon at the party. Everybody went to parties if they weren't dead or Orthodox. He would be there, and she would, and a party had to offer something romantic, not necessarily a conversation. All the boys by now had their bar-mitzvah jackets and slacks to wear. Sandie Berg whinnied around school with a ponytail and white socks, in pink sweaters, pleated plaid skirts. And now Ellen Malkoff had a dress less embarrassing than the baby dress she wore to the Boy Scout dance two years ago. The dress she'd wear to see Michael Gordon at Sandie Berg's party was navy blue, left over from Passover. Like her, dark, a little heavy. Shoes with thick, low Cuban heels. Tan nylon stockings that bagged at knees and ankles from the minute you put them on.

Had to be Mrs. Berg who opened the door, told you and the others who came in your car to go down the stairs after you gave her your coats. There were streamers and shiny wood walls and red-and-white checked linoleum and Sandie—in billows of red taffeta with black velvet bows, like a woman from New Orleans in the novels the librarian couldn't keep from you anymore. Michael Gordon seemed to be on the far side of the red-and-white floor. In a brown tweed bar-mitzvah jacket he was bouncing gently against the wall, falling back against the panels and bobbing up again as Ivan Gold punched him softly on one arm then the other.

Like everyone else, Ellen Malkoff had a present to hand over that her mother had picked out. Sandie had sticky popcorn to offer, and party favors: plastic change purses for girls, miniature pocket knives for boys. The knives were blue-green or dark red outside, and had real metal blades. You could see Joe Corrigliano (Corrigliano's Fruits & Vegetables, Middle Neck Road) take a dark red one and open it, then wheel behind Bill Dooley's shoulder to flick a long splinter out of the wall panel. All the girls' change purses were Day-Glo pink, oval, bendable thick plastic slit across the middle, a little like a huge fuchsia plastic coffee bean. The chain that came out through one end would go around some wrists, not Ellen Malkoff's.

Moving in clumps, the rest of the girls giggled together. Boys coughed in each other's faces. Light slid from bright-coated wall panels to polished linoleum. The hi-fi in the corner, tended by Mr. Berg, produced the big-band noises parents danced to in hotels on the radio. Ellen Malkoff hid her early taste for rhythm 'n' blues like the wrapped Kotex pad in the shoulder bag she'd left with her coat. She leaned against the wall panel next to a chair with a red plastic seat that must have come from a kitchen and watched Don Seitzman march into the corner farthest from the bar and the hi-fi, where Ivan Gold and Judy Greenstine were working up a dance to "Pennsylvania 6-5-0-0-0." A line of boys including Michael Gordon lounged against the wall nearby. Suave enough to be scary in a black-and-white herringbone jacket, Ivan Gold was a full head taller than Don Seitzman, who reached up and tapped him on the shoulder, the way everybody learned to cut in in Social Dancing in sixth grade. "What do you think *you're* doing?" he said upward, loud enough for the whole basement. Ellen Malkoff thought she saw Michael Gordon and the others draw closer together, shoulder to shoulder. They watched without speaking.

The dancers didn't stop shuffling. "Lindy Hop, stupid," they breathed together. They broke apart—her left arm and his right arm flew wide; her right arm went around his waist, his left arm around hers—and turned to face Don Seitzman, dancing a step side by side, smoothly, confidently; but he blocked their way, shaking his head. "I don't think that's right. That's *not* the Lindy Hop"—loud enough to invite the class on all sides to judge.

"Seitzman. *Seitzman.*" Ralph Zelber called him from the stairs. "Come on, Seitzman." On his feet, Ralph Zelber was almost as tall as Ivan Gold. Maybe his sleeve problem made him tolerant—or boys had some way of talking to each other. And he and Don Seitzman probably carpooled together to the party. He took two long strides toward the group in the corner, reached out while Ivan Gold and Judy Greenstine turned to dance face to face again, and hooked a long knobby finger into Don Seitzman's shirt collar. He tugged. Even from behind a clutch of girls in puffy party dresses on the other side of the basement, Ellen Malkoff could see Don Seitzman didn't want to let go. He inched around toward Ralph Zelber and roared, "I know the Lindy Hop. That's not the Lindy Hop."

"The Kensington School Lindy Hop, maybe, Seitzman?" Ralph Zelber, most of whose depths would stay hidden from the crowd for another decade, was putting on some voice like a visitor on Jack Benny. Who would have known him for a mimic, a comic? "You, Seitzman, are without a doubt the Saddle Rock School Lindy Hop maven of all time." The line of boys against the far wall with Michael Gordon among them fell back into separate slouches.

Soon as Mr. Berg turned off the record-player, girls gathered obediently before Sandie for the present-opening. Her grin wavered behind a bright pile of boxes at the end of the bar opposite the hi-fi. Her red, red dress filled the mirror behind the bar. Ellen Malkoff watched Billy Dooley (was his father a policeman—in Queens?) and Joe Corrigliano sidle into the corner to flip through records. "Wayne King?" Corrigliano wailed. That was the year of pink and black. (Ivan Gold was wearing a pink shirt under his black-and-white jacket.) Sandie opened every single pink-and-black present, "*Thank* you!" and squealed the way she would squeal through her Sweet-Sixteen, her bridal shower, her first baby shower. At the fringe of the girls, Ellen Malkoff may have realized that night that she could *not* squeal. Like flapping shirt sleeves, this could shape a life.

After the presents, the cake. It sagged under a garland of pink and yellow roses. Without discussion, Mr. Berg hacked out two extra-large pieces of cake, slapped them on plates that were shoved at boys, then sculpted a delicate slice for Judy Greenstine with more, larger, pink *and* yellow buttercream flowers than any other slice except Sandie's own. Some girl at a party had to have a rose, and Judy Greenstine knew she was that girl. It was a rule like finding one cute boy in a class. Almost the same thing, Ellen Malkoff calculated, because the girl-who-had-to-have-a-rose was probably The Cute Girl. Did *she* know? Did it feel romantic—or too-sweet, and greasy? Mr. Berg carried the empty cake platter, the serving knife, the half-gallon ice cream containers upstairs to the kitchen. Boys who used a piece of birthday cake as heedlessly as a peanut-butter-and-jelly sandwich began to mutter "What do we do next?" Ellen Malkoff fiddled with the change purse she had no pocket for. Girls of the kind who hoped to be cute ones someday were still scraping pink and yellow buttercream frosting off paper plates when Ivan Gold yelled, "Spin-the-Bottle!"

Does everyone remember Spin-the-Bottle? Players on the floor in a circle, alternating boy-girl-boy-girl. The girl who was It—always a girl?—reached into the center of the circle to spin a clean, dry, empty soda bottle on the floor. A brisk, level spin—needed wrist action. In most hands the bottle wobbled, migrated across several squares of linoleum to come to rest with its mouth against some boy's knobby knee like a devoted retriever. The girl who spun the bottle had to cross the circle and kiss the boy the bottle pointed to. A girl who was actually wearing a boy's steel ID bracelet could *interpret* where the bottle really pointed. A loose crowd (all in the same homeroom since kindergarten, or giddy after chocolate cake and Cokes) would jostle more and more with each spin. Only a mean boy would duck aside at the approach of the bottle.

Ivan Gold shouted "Spin-the-Bottle!" and they answered him with grunts and squeals. He ventured "Post Office! Let's do Post Office!"—maybe more than one kiss, maybe out of sight, maybe even in the dark! Ellen Malkoff didn't say a word. After his own bar mitzvah, she remembered, Jimmy Schaeffer snuck a flash camera into the dark room where couples paid out Post Office forfeits: The camera caught Ivan Gold embracing Julianne Penkauer. As though Ellen Malkoff had a color slide on a movie screen propped on the bar, she could see the picture Jimmy Schaeffer showed around school the week after that party. With their faces jammed together, Ivan Gold and Julianne Penkauer didn't look like kids.

"Spin the Bottle." Voices pulled Ivan Gold back. People milled tensely. Ralph Zelber had yanked away the red streamer over the record player, and he was twisting it around Judy Greenstine's neck with more affection than he would be able to confess for at least ten years. If Judy Greenstine ever wore one boy's ID bracelet, she'd have to wear six. Ellen Malkoff couldn't see Michael Gordon. She slid her gleaming change purse under the base of a green lamp on a table against the wall. The table legs moved sideways like loose teeth. She faced the room. As girls dropped paper plates in a garbage can and smoothed their dresses before sitting on the floor, she heard herself say, "I don't want to play Spin-the-Bottle!"

"Come on," several said.

"I won't *play* Spin-the-Bottle." This was Ellen Malkoff, not screaming, but loud enough to be heard. More than one person sneered, "It's just a game." Were her hands fists at her sides? Did the folds of the navy-blue taffeta skirt cover them? She didn't know. She felt the mob around her in the Bergs' basement prepare to split into three factions: Convince her, Ignore her, Report her.

Michael Gordon stepped out of a phalanx of boys with his right hand conspicuously in his jacket pocket. The mass of a moment before divided neatly to leave the two of them, Michael Gordon and Ellen Malkoff, alone in the center of the floor, like the instructors in Social Dancing.

What happened next happened slowly. At least it is remembered slowly. Michael Gordon challenged her. "Won't play Spin-the-Bottle?"

"You can't make me" came out automatically. Not romantic. Just what you say. He took another step toward her and seized her left arm on the inside with his left hand. He clutched it against his body, parallel to the floor. His right hand rose out of his jacket pocket, in it the miniature knife he had received as a favor, open to a blade no more than two inches long. He jabbed the little knife into the muscle of her forearm and pulled it toward her wrist. Pulled it slowly but fiercely, with the kind of gesture you use to scrape a finish line in wet sand with a stick. She didn't hear a word or a sigh. She didn't turn away as you turn from the doctor, not to see the needle. She watched the small blade slightly curved on both sides, almost the shape of a candle flame. None of the bright light bouncing around that basement bounced back from that blade as it moved. Perhaps she took in the knife blade so intensely that she had no time for pain.

Ellen Malkoff didn't struggle. Why ever not? Michael Gordon was nothing like as imposing as Jimmy Schaeffer, who pushed his handkerchief at her without a word when he caught her wiping her nose on her sleeve in fifth grade, then, unaccountably, asked her to the Boy Scouts' dance. And she was much taller than Julianne Penkauer, who was not even the shortest girl in class. Also, Michael Gordon needed one hand to manipulate the knife, which left him only one hand to hold her arm—his left hand on her left arm, and she was left-handed, which was almost embarrassing. Strong for a girl. But she didn't move. She did not move.

Michael Gordon dropped the arm and snapped his blade back inside the blue-green case. "That's what you get," he said. "Next time you play."

"Who says," she said, mechanically. Now *she* was holding

her left arm from the inside near the elbow, parallel to the floor. Where he'd held it? Blood dark as the red of Joe Corrigliano's knife welled up slowly along the line Michael Gordon had drawn. A thick line, with wiggles in it. She felt no need to hurry. She watched her arm.

Once blood began to ooze over her forearm and down, over her right thumb, she thought of the navy-blue dress. What blood could do to a good dress. What going home with blood on her good dress would do to her. She pushed her left arm further from her body and looked curiously at the red-and-white tiled floor beneath it. A familiar pair of tan shoes stopped just beyond where blood could spatter. "What are you going to do?" Don Seitzman said. "You have to do something. What are you going to do?"

"It doesn't hurt." Ellen Malkoff turned and ran up the stairs. As she ran she closed her right hand over the mess on her forearm.

The bathroom opposite the top of the stairs had been left open and lighted so no one would have to ask where to go during the party. Backs to her, Mr. and Mrs. Berg leaned toward each other, facing the kitchen sink. That moment, Mrs. Berg slapped her right hip against Mr. Berg's left thigh. They were laughing as the bathroom door closed. It locked.

Cold water. A paper guest towel. You couldn't ask Mrs. Berg for a Band-Aid; she was not a known mother. You couldn't say you had to call your parents to come get you. Your father was a ride for three other girls who lived on the old side of town. You would have to go back to the party and read record labels while Spin-the-Bottle finished. Was this house old enough to have *Coronet* magazines lying around the basement that you could read in a corner? When she walked down the basement steps again, no one asked why she had a paper guest towel on her arm.

Mothers must have talked to each other the next day, a

Susan Holahan

Sunday. Michael Gordon must have been ordered to apologize. On notepaper left over from his bar mitzvah, in place of "Thank you for the fountain pen," he wrote, "I'm sorry I did that," in one line as rough as the line he cut in Ellen Malkoff's arm. When his note arrived in the mail like an invitation, she realized cute went only so far. She never tried to speak to him again. Not even Don Seitzman ever mentioned the party.

Exactly a year later, necking for the first time, Ellen Malkoff suspected she was *enjoying* the same kind of passionate attention Michael Gordon had paid her for one long moment at Sandie Berg's party. Trembling in the front seat of the car that belonged to a date old enough to drive, she didn't know what would happen next. She had no name for what she was feeling. She was shaking, and very, very busy, inside something that placed a wall between her and—outside. Time wasn't time. This was nothing you could possibly stop; or there was no you to stop it.

Into high school the scar on her arm stayed pinkish and puffy. Finally it paled and shrank. In college, IKE remained president. His niece played bridge most days in the common room with the daughter of his attorney general, the same man who—Ellen Malkoff had by now read it— moved the Rosenbergs' execution *up* three hours so they wouldn't die on the Sabbath. One night in her junior year she sat through a student play. Behind her in the dark auditorium a woman whispered, "That sophomore—the one who's the son? There's a story about him. He's an orphan or something." The young man's face under lights stayed with Ellen Malkoff for years like the face of the pale, serious child—the older of two brothers; they would be raised by a childless, "progressive" couple—caught by a Speed Graphic at a prison wall in 1953. Later that year, reading for Social Psychology 206 about the Asch-Witkin social-pressure experiments, she returned again and again,

92

sensing kinship, to those subjects who resisted the group perception: They saw the truth and they insisted on what they saw: They were *right*, but difficult, uncomfortable, unsuccessful.

Nixon was president when a consciousness-raising group asked her, "That scar on your arm, where'd you get that?"

"I wouldn't play Spin-the-Bottle, once," she tried.

"Come on," they said.

"It was a tougher neighborhood I grew up in than people think." But she laughed when she said it and the two women who were leaving their husbands for each other, and into sharing everything, accused her of bad faith: That couldn't be the whole truth. She obviously wasn't ready to let her sisters help her understand her experience. If she didn't leave the group, *they* would.

While Nixon was still president, everything from groceries to child care turned cooperative. It occurred to Ellen Malkoff—who never really turned communal, never could share gracefully, ice cream or her only child—to remember that no one at Sandie Berg's party moved to stop Michael Gordon when he attacked her. (She'd never thought "attacked" before. She used the word "cut.") They all had learned from birth to keep to themselves. Girls wore girdles at twelve. You didn't discuss politics with strangers. No one in the basement looked up from Spin-the-Bottle when she walked down the stairs with paper wadded to her arm.

When, for the first time, the new president is younger than you are, and head of the cohort that has always hugged and shared, everything changes. Nothing is ever the same again, except a two-inch scar that rises almost white along your left arm, starting a few inches from your elbow. You've always thought of it—rounded at the end toward your wrist, irregular along both sides—as a worm. You don't think of it often now. You haven't had to explain it for years.

The pain was out there waiting but we didn't have to know about it. We suffered the accidents of our lives dumbly as we obeyed the kind of rules that came from nowhere and required girls to brave winter dates with only frozen nylon stockings on legs scraped raw by dull razors. That Ellen Malkoff did what she could, then: She said out loud what she knew. Now forgive her.

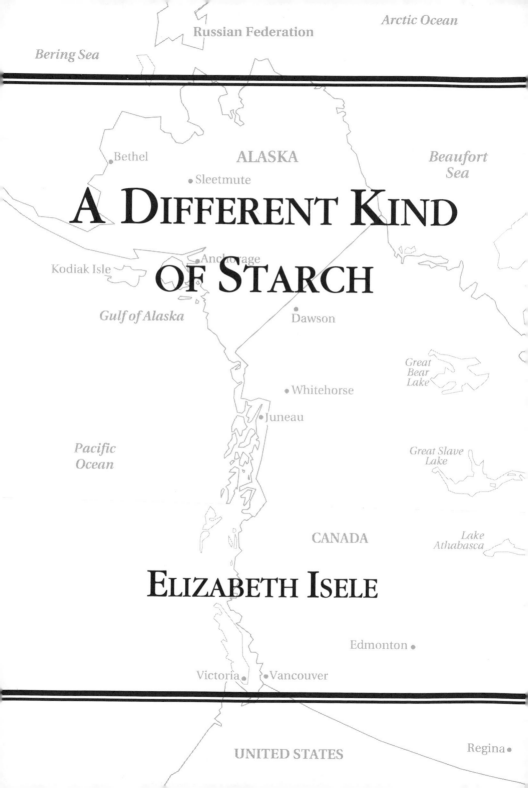

A DIFFERENT KIND OF STARCH

ELIZABETH ISELE

Elizabeth Isele has been involved in publishing for near-
ly thirty years. She was an acquisitions editor at Harper &
Row and later managing editor of the juvenile imprints T.
Y. Crowell and J. B. Lippincott. Ms. Isele currently operates
her own firm, which encompasses a range of literary ser-
vices from editorial assistance and book design to market-
ing and financial analysis. In addition, she is a creative
writing instructor at Wesleyan University.

Ms. Isele has written nine children's books, including
four on Native Americans, *Pooks*, and *The Frog Princess*.
The following selection will be featured in the forthcoming
collection *Grand Mothers: A Multicultural Anthology of
Poems, Reminiscences, and Short Stories about the Keepers of
Our Traditions*, edited by Nikki Giovanni, to be published
in August by Henry Holt and Company.

Ms. Isele has four children and has traveled extensively,
especially in the American West. She lives in Connecticut.

My grandfather used to call her "Little Pistol." Nana was barely five feet tall. She wore a size three shoe, and that was only after she had married and had two children. Before then, she wore a size one. Her shoes had to be custom-made.

All Nana's clothes were custom-made, too, in beautiful colors and exquisitely textured fabrics. Hats (half-veiled), dresses, shoes, stockings, handbags, and gloves—everything matched. She always wore gloves. Cotton in summer and suede in winter: the softest suede I ever felt. As passionately as she loved dressing up, she always told me, "It's not the clothes but what's underneath that counts."

Her childhood home, a brownstone in New York City, was furnished with English antiques and oriental carpets. Oil paintings hung in gold frames on silk-covered walls. Warm gas light and music filled the rooms, and there were servants to cook, clean, polish silver, do laundry, groom the horses, shovel out stalls, oil hand-tooled carriages, light the fires in winter, and ladle lemonade for the iceman in summer.

When Nana was ten she demanded a cart for Banjo, her favorite pony. From that time on, instead of riding in an elegant carriage through Central Park with her parents, her beautiful older sister, and handsome younger brother, she took up the reins and drove her pony cart.

Every Sunday morning she gave Banjo a flick of the whip and they streaked out after the family carriage. Back and forth—first behind, then alongside, then in front—Nana and Banjo raced along like lunatics. Her mother was appalled.

"She really is quite a handful," her mother decided and sent Nana off to private schools, hoping they might make a "lady" of her. The schools had stodgy names like Miss Porter's and Emma Walker's, and Nana was bored.

"Art history, manners, and deportment," she said, remembering the curriculum with disgust. "What good are grace and decorum if you can't have any fun?"

Her last year of formal education was at Chalfonte-Haddon Hall, a "finishing school." "Finish my foot," she said. "I have hardly begun."

That fall, she met my grandfather at a Halloween costume ball. She had come dressed as a milkmaid and he as a farmer. Nana said, "We started dancing that night and never stopped."

His family were not at all sure Nana was the right woman for their son to marry. They were strict Methodists, and Nana's family were Lutherans. Lutheran was synonymous with libertine to them, and Nana was, after all, Nana.

Her family, however, were delighted. They felt marriage might be just the thing to calm Nana down. I don't think it calmed down either one of them. I met my grandfather for the first time on an August afternoon so hot that the air shimmered above our driveway. I had been waiting hours for them on the front porch and raced down to meet their long, black Packard. My grandfather stepped out first, wearing a seersucker suit and tie, shiny shoes, and a Panama hat with a blue and white band to match his suit. I had expected a farmer; I hadn't realized he would be just as custom-made as Nana.

He was so tall I could not see his face. He reached out his arm to me, scooped me up close and smiled. With his other hand he pulled an ice cream cone out of his jacket pocket. "For you," he said. "I hope you like chocolate."

"We're driving out West," said Nana. "We want to see the prairie and the deserts, ghost towns and old gold mines, and cowboys and Indians, if there are any left."

Nana sent me picture postcards with hastily scribbled notes such as "On the trail in Sante Fe" and "Beautiful turquoise jewelry here in New Mexico." Grandpa took her picture next to a giant cactus in Arizona, and they mailed an envelope full of buffalo hair from Wyoming. Nana learned to weave from a Navajo woman in Taos, and they barreled down treacherous dirt roads in Colorado in hot pursuit of some cowpunchers' chuckwagon. She didn't much like branding steers at the roundup, but Nana loved panning for gold outside of Sacramento.

They tied a burlap water bag over the front of the radiator and drove the Packard through Death Valley. In a ghost town, they had someone take their picture in front of the saloon. Grandpa looked a little self-conscious in his sheepskin chaps and ten-gallon hat. Nana's cowboy boots were so big she looked somewhat wobbly, and her ten-gallon hat squished the tops of her ears, but she was beaming.

When I listened to "The Lone Ranger" on our old Philco radio, I pictured my grandmother charging over the hills after desperadoes shouting, "Hi-ho, Banjo, away!"

She sent me cowboy boots and a pair of six-shooters with red and green leather holsters. I wore them morning, noon, and night. My mother was aghast.

Finally, after months on the road, they came back East for Christmas. We were waiting at their house when they drove in. The Packard looked a little the worse for wear, but Nana looked grand. Still wearing her cowboy hat, she had attached a little half-veil to it for the holidays.

On Christmas Eve, Nana taught me how to string popcorn and cranberries for her tree. We sat on the big down sofa—the one whose pillows were plumped at least three times a day. At the other end of the living room, Grandpa played Christmas carols on the Victrola for my brother and sister. The draperies were open just enough for us to see frost etching the windowpanes.

My mother, Nana's daughter, was not back yet. Someone had telephoned her from the station bar, and she had gone out looking for my father. Sometimes she found him, most times she didn't.

I never knew my mother well. I still don't. She felt that children should be seen and not heard. Appearances were important to her, and she wanted us to be "seen" perfectly. We were scrubbed and starched. Even our underwear was starched. She had some peculiar economies. One of them was recycling old sheets by making them into underpants for my sister and me. Actually, they looked more like boxer shorts, so she sewed eyelet lace around the legs. I hated them.

Above all, we were to be quiet. Sometimes my mother spent the entire day in her bedroom with the shades drawn. She had terrible headaches, and my thundering around the house in my cowboy boots firing caps from my six-shooters did not help. Her silences frightened me, and I was desperate for some sound—even my own.

I heard the pantry door swing open and Frances, Nana's cook, carried hot cinnamon cider and cocoa into the living room. We smelled her Christmas stollen and gingerbread cookies baking in the kitchen. "Soon," she said.

Sitting close to Nana, I tried not to scratch where my starched underwear itched. We were watching Grandpa clip the candles onto the branches, when suddenly a bolt of lightning ripped into the old beech tree beside the house. The bolt ricocheted off the tree and burst through the window by the sofa. It shot across the living room past the Victrola and out the window directly opposite the one it had entered. I was terrified. Nana hugged me tight and said, "My goodness! We almost didn't have to light the candles on the tree this year, did we?"

It had nothing to do with the lightning, but my grandfather died shortly after that Christmas. Nana missed him terribly. She said, "It's all these trappings. I just can't find him in all these trappings."

She decided to move to California—not to Death Valley or to Gold Rush territory, but to a little beach house they had seen together in Santa Monica. "I can picture you cart-ing a few things across country in a covered wagon and settling down here by the water," Grandpa had said.

When she came to say good-bye, Nana's arms were loaded with big boxes. "Wait downstairs," she said as she struggled through my bedroom door.

Finally she called, and I bolted upstairs. Clothes were carefully arranged all over my bed. She had put a hat on my pillow. There was a beautiful blue and white dress, and a purse and matching shoes with light blue socks tucked inside. And lying next to all of this were six pairs of soft Carters' underpants with ponies printed all over them. "For a very special cowgirl," she said, reaching out to touch my cheek. "With love from Nana."

When it was time to go to college, I chose one in California. My mother and father thought I was crazy. "One year," they said. "We'll pay for one year, and then you'll come back East where you belong."

I never went home again. I spent many school holidays with Nana at the beach house. The Christmas Eve when she was 74, we opened presents around a table-top tree with tiny candles on it. She looked at me and said, "How about New Year's in Alaska? I'd like to hear more about that Iditarod."

EXPECTING

TASHA BLAINE

T asha Blaine was born in New York City. A free-lance writer, she is currently studying at Barnard College, where she is majoring in English. Ms. Blaine also studied abroad, at the Institute of European Studies, Milan, Italy.

Ms. Blaine lives in New York City. The following selection is her first published piece of fiction. It is from a work in progress.

She stood holding a wooden spoon streaked with spaghetti sauce, telling us we had to move because she was pregnant. She cupped a hand over her stomach, and I noticed that the top button of her jeans was undone. I wanted to close it. She leaned against the counter, sighed, and tasted the sauce. My eyes roamed around the kitchen, not wanting to look at her open jeans. We had walls the color of rust in that first kitchen. And a table shaped like an oversized spool of thread, the wood dry and rough. The shelf paper in the cabinets had curled up showing a glue-stained underside. Jars of molasses had left thick rings on the countertop, and the door of the refrigerator was splattered with orange juice. She turned her back on me, my brother, and my sister and faced the stove. Hunched over the pot, she stirred the sauce, then reached down to lower the flame. We didn't ask any questions.

We packed. Days of folding, stacking, wrapping, taping, tying. Black newspaper ink covered our hands. Red rings were left on my fingers by the string. I listened to the sounds change as our belongings were stripped from beds and shelves; as the walls became bare, the rooms echoed sounds that were once muffled. Our apartment became a cave with blank walls scarred by nails and tape, our dirt-stained handprints. I pushed out the last box, my six-year-old face reddening from the effort. My family stood together in the doorway watching dust-filled sunbeams stream through the empty living room. Then my mother shut the door.

My new room glowed blue. A blue bulb shone from the ceiling, and I called to my mother, "It's just like a disco" as I spun around in the color. She watched me, hands resting on her taut stomach; then, laughing, she stepped into the light. I twirled around my mother until she became a flash of movement, a hand rubbing a belly, a foot moving forward. Overcome with dizziness, I fell and felt the thrill of nausea in my mouth as I lay and watched the blue ceiling spin.

The new kitchen was white, paint thick and bubbled. A piece of plaster hung from the ceiling, and I wanted to knock it down. The shelf paper was already peeling.

Names written in pencil, pen, and marker covered the inside wall of my closet. Black lines of feet and inches with a name by each mark climbed up the door, a ladder of growth. I ran my hand over the marks and names, closing my eyes to feel the people who once lived here, but I felt nothing but the texture of the wood. Opening my eyes, I saw one black sock left behind in a corner.

A long hallway led to my mother's room, dark even in the middle of the day. I stood at the edge of the darkness with my eyes on the sun at the far end, afraid of what lay in between. Clenching my fists, I ducked my head and plunged forward, heart beating hard.

The silence of the hall surrounded me, but inside the pounding filled my ears. I was plowing, hands wet, legs hot and itching, with my head bent forward so I could push through the darkness. I emerged from the tunnel with gray dust hanging off the bottoms of my white socks, still feeling some creature's hands around my ankles. The air reached my lungs, and as I uncurled my fists I saw my dented palms, skin almost broken where my nails had pressed in.

We unpacked, untied, and unwrapped. My skin was as dry as the newspaper filling the boxes. My mother placed her books on shelves built into the living-room walls. She carefully slid them in one after the other, pausing to read a title, sometimes rubbing a cover. We called rooms, my sister Iona and I in the bigger one, my brother Miles alone in the smaller. Dishes were rinsed and given places in the cabinet.

Beds were made, and Iona and I covered a wall in our room with a poster my mother had bought at a museum of peasants dancing in shoes that curled up at the toes.

The next morning I realized that my mother had screwed in a new light bulb. It shone a clean light, revealing cracked, smudged walls. I leaned over the side of my bunk bed and stretched out toward the light, wanting to unscrew the bulb, make it softer and dimmer. But I couldn't reach it, and my sister Iona pushed me back onto the bed, telling me blue wasn't the right color for a home, and she wondered who had lived in the apartment before us.

Iona hummed at night after we moved. I hung from my bed and watched her below, her hands pressed together, eyes closed, legs crossed. "I'm communing with the spirits," she told me and kept humming, making the boards of my bunk vibrate. I pictured Iona with her straight black hair tightly braided and a line of red paint smoothed over each cheek. As she rocked, I could hear the swoosh of fringe hanging from a buffalo skin shirt.

Iona was speaking with her ancestors, the ancient American Indians. This was an ability only she had because of our different fathers. Iona inherited her gift from her grandmother, Regina, with the thick ebony hair. My sister hummed, and Miles came into our room as if the droning noise were calling him. He listened in awe as Iona spoke in the voice of an ancient chief. I wondered why Miles wasn't speaking to the Indians himself since he had the same father as Iona, but I kept quiet and listened to her stories. Sitting still, I closed my eyes halfway and watched the darkness until I finally saw the spirits dancing. They looked like wisps of my mother's cigarette smoke.

A few weeks later Iona went to the eye doctor, and the night she came home with her glasses she began to talk about what she saw through their thick lenses. She saw all the way to other planets. People walked on the moon, wearing robes of white so that nobody on earth could see them moving about. Iona sat in the darkness of our room, seeing everything through glass; the building across the way lost its brick front and became a dollhouse with three walls. She could see families in their apartments in front of television sets, talking on phones, and taking baths. The family on the second floor left piles of clothes all over the living room, the woman on the sixth lived alone in a leopard-spotted apartment.

Iona described these homes when my mother was out late and I didn't know where she was. I imagined her walking home from the 157th Street train stop, passing under the tree with the banana-shaped pods. She walked down the hill of cracked cement, her clicking heels the only sound on our dark street. My mother's steps echoed as she passed beneath the banana tree, and that's where I pictured him grabbing her, covering her mouth with his hand and crushing her neck in the loop of his arm. She fell onto the sidewalk, a foot hanging over the curb, her toe touching the street. The lamp above her, brighter than the one in my room, shone onto my mother's fallen body. He padded away, his rubber-soled shoes absorbing the sound of his footfalls, the strap of my mother's purse wrapped around his hand.

Iona began telling stories of the people across the street, and I forgot about the banana tree, and just when the woman in the leopard-spotted apartment was opening the door to a handsome stranger, I heard a key in our lock. The hinges creaked, and my mother laughed softly in the foyer with her boyfriend. Keys jingled, the closet door opened. They walked down the long hallway. When my mother's bedroom door shut, I heard a light switch flip, another giggle, and a sigh. I heard drawers sliding open, silence, and then his distant cough. Iona's voice had stopped, and she breathed heavily as though she were sleeping. I turned toward the wall, angry and relieved.

*　　　*　　　*

My mother woke us before it was light, before the sun even hit the edges of the sky. She pulled my hair when she braided it, lifting my scalp. Iona and I dressed, and my mother went back into the kitchen. My mother's boyfriend was sitting at our table when I walked into the room, his eyes bloodshot, head hanging low over his eggs and grits. My brother slapped his leg as though it were a drum as he ate. Then he reached over to hit me on the back of my head. I screamed and kicked his shins. Iona told us to stop, and my brother grabbed a fistful of her hair, pulling her head back until her chin pointed to the ceiling. "Look, I have my own private horn," Miles said while she wailed. My mother's boyfriend poured salt over his plate, head falling deeper into his food while we fought and ran around him.

We were dropped at Marisol and Jasmine's apartment, two teenagers who lived below us. Jasmine had started coming up to talk to my mother, who let her smoke cigarettes and even gave away some of her own. Winstons in a soft pack. Jasmine talked about her boyfriend, the man who sold fruit at the Foodtown on Broadway, how he used to stare at her when she came in, how he used to give her free mangoes, and finally how he asked her out. "My father doesn't like him because he's older," she told my mother as she inhaled smoke. "But he's got a purple Corvette and is he fine!" They laughed together and rocked back in their chairs.

Jasmine had told my mother she'd watch us when my mother went to work in the health-food store downtown. But it was really her sister Marisol who took care of us. Jasmine placed a pillow on her windowsill, resting her head on her forearms. She watched for her boyfriend's car, and when it pulled up to the corner he pushed his horn, which played the "Woody Woodpecker" theme. "Oh, Miguel is here!" she screamed and came in from the window. She threw the pillow on the bed and paused for a moment in front of the mirror with a smile, then she flew out the front door.

Marisol stayed with me while Iona and Miles watched television in the other room. She rolled my hair in pink foam curlers, then wrapped my head in a scarf. Hours later, she combed it out and cried, *"Ayyy, que linda. Mommy, look how cute she is."* Her mother pinched my cheeks and told me she hoped my blonde hair never changed color.

She led me into the kitchen where she was making food to sell to the Spanish restaurant on the corner. I watched as she put a pork sandwich on a grill and pressed it like a dry cleaner. She cut it into three pieces and told me to take it to Iona and Miles. The three of us sat in front of the television, careful to keep the crumbs from falling into the furniture.

A rug hung on the wall, above the couch in the living room. A scene of the Last Supper. I stretched my arm up to the rug, rubbing it while I watched television. Marisol and Jasmine's mother dusted her plastic-coated lamps. We lifted our feet and held them in the air while she swept the floor. She mopped, and the room became lemon-scented.

The brothers came home in the late afternoon. Two brothers, older than Marisol and Jasmine. Tall, the prickly beginnings of facial hair on their chins and above their lips. They played pool in the other room. The click-click of balls, the drawing of breath, and then its release when a ball rolled into a pocket was mysterious and new to me. I peeked through the slit of the barely opened door, seeing strong hands rubbing blue chalk onto the tip of a cue stick, grinding it. A soft stream of blue dust fell slowly to the floor. Pushing the door open just an inch more, I hoped they would see me.

"Come here, little blondie," one of the brothers called to me, leaning down, bringing his face level with mine. His features grew large up close, magnified, rich brown eyes framed by thick lashes, sweat on his upper lip like a mist.

"You wanna watch? You could sit on the stool over there," the other brother said, pointing. I sat, perched on my stool like a referee. The balls rolled over the green table, flashes of color. A brother called a pocket, eyed the angle, held the cue steady, and then shot. A click and then the soft drop of satisfaction. Then they were down to the eight ball, and a brother took the shot. The ball flew, black against green, to a pocket and fell, disappearing into the table. "I win," he said, lifting an eyebrow and the opposite corner of his mouth.

"You never called the pocket," the other brother spat back.

"You know I did."

"You did not call no pocket. Did he, little blondie?" But his brother had already left the pool table.

"Didn't I call it, little one?" he said as he walked toward me. He picked me up with his two hands, my waist reduced to nothing under their size. "I call this one right here, right here. I won because I got little blondie down the pocket." He sat me on the table, standing in front of me. My legs stuck out, and he stood between them. His hand touched my newly coiffed hair, the other held my thigh. "Ohh, *rubia, rubia, rubia.*" One finger glided down my cheek, grazed my neck, hooked into the collar of my shirt. "*Rubia, rubia.* Little blonde one."

I squirmed away from him and slid off the table. I laughed. "I could never fit into one of those pockets," I joked. And then slipped out of the room. Found Iona and Miles leaning on Jasmine's pillow in her window, watching the street six floors below.

I stood at the foot of my mother's bed that evening, patiently waiting for her to glance up and see me there, a vision in my curled and sprayed hair. She continued reading, and I wasn't sure if she even knew I was in the room. I called to her over and over, but her face sank deeper into the crease of her novel. When she finally looked up she laughed and said, "My God, look at you. Your hair is all done up!" Before she flipped the page to begin a new chapter, she told me to wash it out because no six-year-old should go around with a hairstyle.

I turned to the mirror over her bureau and patted my stiff hair. It wasn't the style that I had liked so much, but Marisol's hands gently separating my hair into sections, pulling it straight, and then running a comb easily through it. She nudged my head forward to lift up a strand and wet it with the same sprayer my mother used on our plants. Marisol curled each section slowly around the pink foam logs, one by one, covering my whole head. She tied a scarf over the curlers and used the tips of her fingers to tuck in the loose strands around my forehead.

I wouldn't miss the height and the curl my hair now had, but I wished for the exclamations of surprise that had come from Marisol and her mother when my hair was unwrapped like a present. I was something new at that moment. I was being unveiled.

I turned on the water in the bathtub and leaned over the side. Closing my eyes, I let the water run through my hair, carrying the curl and sticky spray down the drain. I squeezed water out of my hair and wrapped it in a towel like a turban. Sitting on the edge of the tub, I took off my socks and put my feet under the water. As I reached to turn off the faucet, the towel unfolded and fell to the floor. I stood in front of the mirror, hair straight and dark.

"Oh, that's better. You're a clean bug now," my mother said, seeing me at the foot of her bed again. I walked to the side of the bed, where my mother held her book. Leaning over, I could read over her shoulder. I saw the black print and longed for pictures. My mother's stomach rose like a mountain underneath her sheet. I thought about running my hand over it, flattening it into a plane.

"You're blocking my light," she said, not looking up. As I

climbed over her legs, my stomach brushed hers and for the first time I felt its hardness, the tautness, an unbreakable balloon. I lay beside my mother while she read. Lights went off a few hours later, and I stayed in bed. In the darkness my hand gripped her wrist, and I slipped into a dream.

It was hot, humid, heavy August. Iona and Miles had found a mulberry tree on our corner, and I saw legs and arms sticking out of the branches. They swung their limbs in slow motion through the heat rising from the sidewalk. I walked toward them, calling for berries. Plump purple berries growing in the middle of New York. The gray cement was splattered with fruit that had been crushed by the shoes of passersby.

Bouncing on a branch and shaking the leaves, my brother yelled, "Look out below!" A shower of fruit fell into my open hands. Iona leaned back on her branch, curving her body to its knots and grooves. With one hand across her stomach, she stared at pieces of sky through the green leaves. I popped berries into my mouth one by one like bits of smooth chocolate.

I left Iona and Miles in the tree, and went upstairs to wash my sticky hands. I called to my mother and when she didn't answer I ran through the black hallway. In her bedroom the sheet was on the floor. The windows were open, but it was still so hot that there was a wet spot on the bed where my mother had just lain.

I found her leaning over the toilet, gripping the bowl with her hands. Her body suddenly lunged forward, and a deep guttural sound echoed off the tile of the wall. She panted, sucking in air. Thick clumps of hair stuck to her forehead, and she rubbed her head against her shoulder to push them off her face.

Terrified, I called out to her.

"Go away!" she gasped and waved a hand toward the door.

I ran to her and pressed myself against her, my stomach stretched over her back, arms around her. She breathed heavily, and I moved with each breath, rising and sinking into her spine. I peered over her shoulder, wondering if the baby would come out of her mouth.

My mother let go of the toilet and crawled toward the wall. I slid off of her, and with a washcloth wiped her sticky mouth and forehead. I held a glass of water to her mouth. She grabbed my hand, gulping, and some of the water streamed down her chin to her neck, where I caught it with the washcloth. Laying her hand on the curve of her belly, my mother closed her eyes. I wanted to push on her hand and dent her belly, to squeeze her like a tube of toothpaste until the baby came out and my mother could button her pants again.

Later I sat on the couch. My mother was sleeping with her door closed and I was afraid she might choke in her sleep, so I listened. The apartment made noises on its own, the hum of the refrigerator, the thump of someone walking on the floor above, and the sound of music from a car passing below. For a moment the music was inside the apartment, beating loud; then it faded into the walls as the car moved down the street. I listened to the soft movements of our home, straining to hear any sounds of danger from my mother's room.

My mother came out of her room when the front door slammed, as Iona and Miles came in. She smiled, a hint of red on her cheeks. Stretching, she yawned. My mother looked dry and rested, the sweat and water gone. Her hair was twisted and pinned back tightly. She was wearing a floral print dress and sandals with thick cork heels. Iona smiled and walked toward her, putting her hand out to touch the dress. Miles asked if she was going out, and she said we were all going out. To a potluck at Jim and Gail's to discuss nuclear freeze. We moaned, remembering the old bookstore on 107th Street that she used to take us to, with stairs that led down as though into a basement. The meetings had lasted forever, voices droning, merging. Then one voice loud and passionate would break through. My mother's old boyfriend had taken us to those meetings, and it was his voice that paralyzed the room. My mother would glow when he spoke. Chin held high, eyes wet, she saw only him at the front of the room.

There was more to do at Jim and Gail's. Adults milled around the food, holding plates and forks as they stood on line. Laughing and touching each other's shoulders. There was salad, roast chicken, baked ziti, pesto, homemade applesauce, spicy yellow rice, all in bowls brought by the guests. Jugs of red and white wine took up the corner table, which was covered with paper. A bucket of ice kept the beer cold.

Iona and I found two other sisters and the four of us wandered around the apartment, going through drawers in the empty bedrooms, opening medicine cabinets and hall closets. We heard the crowd down the hall and the soft rhythm of jazz. Beers were opened. The bottle caps flipped off and flew to the floor. We raced among the guests' feet, seized the caps, and compared individual hoards.

My mother called us in when the lights in the living room were turned off. All the chairs faced a white sheet hanging on the wall. Miles waved his hand in front of the slide projector, and it flew across the sheet. The first slide popped in, displaying a pink and blue graph on the wall. The speaker began to talk about percentages and taxes. He spoke softly and steadily, describing radiation and the nuclear winter. I pinched my sister, and we tried to slip away, but my mother pulled us back. "Watch and listen. This is important," she whispered.

I stopped listening and the colored graphs began to blur. I felt Miles swing his leg and slap his thigh as though the music were still on. The last slide flipped in, the finale, a huge mushroom cloud bursting through the sky. A moment of silence followed, then words of disgust. "This is what our government is doing?" or "I pay taxes for this?" The lights came on. Coffee was brewed and the table cleared for a new series of bowls. Cookies, cake, and pies. A line formed around the table. Music played on the stereo and the laughing began.

I wanted to go. The other sisters had left. Iona had pulled a book out of her pocket and found a corner. I asked my mother to leave, pulling at her dress, but she continued talking. I pulled again and said her name, Silvia.

"Let me just finish my coffee," she said brushing the top of my head.

"Yeah, but how long will that take?"

"Just a few more minutes. Just give me a few more minutes." Then she was lost again in conversation.

I found Miles asleep on top of the jackets in the bedroom. I walked in and lay down next to him. Iona sat on the highest peak of belongings, lifting her book up to the lamp. My mother must have found the three of us there, twisted around each other, half buried under jackets.

The doorbell rang as I lay in my own bed in the morning, thinking of getting up. The house was quiet as always on a Saturday, and the sound startled me. I climbed down from my bunk, leaving Iona asleep below. I opened the door to a woman wearing a black tank top, gray now from too many washings, and jeans that ended just above her ankles. Her short hair was greased down to frame her forehead, flattened strands caught in a curl. She walked right past me, and I smelled cocoa butter.

"Where's your mama?" she asked, heading into my room. Then she came back out and headed down the black hallway to my mother's room. I couldn't see her in the darkness, but I could hear her flipflops slap on the floor.

Iona came out and stood behind me, with a hand on my shoulder. I knew the woman was opening my mother's door, because the light from her room made a triangle in the hallway.

"What do you think you're doing with my man?" I heard her say to my mother, and then the door closed. I moved to sit in the dark corridor, keeping my foot in the light of the living room so I would be safe.

"Your man?" my mother asked. "What are you talking about? I don't even know who you are."

"You think you're some fancy white woman who can just come and take my man, and you think I'm gonna stand for it? It's always the white women trying to steal our men, come into our neighborhoods and steal our men. Well, I am here to tell you to just forget it. He ain't never coming back to see you again."

My mother was silent, not a word or even a sigh. The door opened all the way and there was a perfect rectangle of light in the hallway.

The woman strode past me and Iona. I tried to grab the back of her flipflop but missed. Iona followed her.

"Get out. This isn't your house, and you don't know anything about my mother," Iona shouted at the woman, who turned around and stopped, looking my sister in the eye.

"Girl, you don't know anything at all. I pity you. I really do."

My sister stood with her arms crossed, a solid wall. I quivered behind her. She matched the woman, staring back into her eyes without a word. The woman swung around and stalked out the door, holding her stomach tight and her back straight.

Iona crumpled when the door closed, folding into herself. She walked in circles around the foyer, clenching her fists. With one foot she stepped into the darkness of the hallway, pointing to my mother's door, paused, and with-

117

drew it. She went into our room, got into bed, and closed her eyes. "Iona," I said, shaking her. She ignored me and moved further under the sheet. She pretended to sleep, as if she had never waked up at all that morning.

Still in my pajamas, I grabbed my pillow and left the apartment. I went down the stairs to Marisol and Jasmine's. Outside their door, I stopped to listen. I heard voices and imagined Marisol cooking me breakfast so that we could eat together in front of Saturday morning cartoons. Click and a ball was shot; Marisol's brother laughed. I took my finger off the bell and stepped away from the door.

Sitting on the top step on our floor, I could see down to the fifth floor, but they couldn't see me. I watched the door, waiting for the brothers to leave. Their mother cleaned on Saturdays, so I knew the house would smell like detergent.

Finally the door opened below, and the two brothers came out with their father. They joked in front of the elevator and I waited patiently for it to come. Their words were spoken quickly, in Spanish. I thought I heard *rubia*, and I darted back behind the railing. But the elevator came and they piled into it.

I counted the floors the elevator must be traveling, and then I walked down the stairs. I rang the bell and Jasmine opened the door. She saw me, smiled, and pulled me inside. Marisol was sweeping, and she told me to sit on her bed until she finished. Later she poured me a bowl of Lucky Charms, and we sat together in front of the television.

My sister shook me awake the night before I was to start first grade. The bare bulb went on. It was so dark outside I could see my reflection in the window. I told Iona my mother couldn't be having the baby now. I looked down at my school clothes laid out over a chair, and told my older sister it just wasn't the right time. She kept calling to me to get up, but I wouldn't answer. I held a pillow tight against my face. My breath became lighter, a mist creeping through my constricted throat. Iona said my name again, and I turned on my stomach, sinking into the bed, weak from lack of air. My mouth was blocked by the sheet and the mattress.

When my mother started screaming in her room I wondered why she didn't go to the hospital like other mothers. She howled, and I couldn't understand why she had chosen a midwife instead of a doctor. Another scream, and I pulled the sheet over myself. Putting my hands over my ears, I hummed. A soft buzz began in my head as I fantasized that my mother was in a hospital.

She feels the first contraction and calmly picks up the phone to call the doctor. Yes, I am ready, doctor. Yes, I'll meet you at the hospital. At the tone, she dials again, this time asking Marisol to come up and watch us while she leaves quietly in the middle of the night. We sleep, and Marisol gets into my mother's bed. My mother's boyfriend rings the bell and appears, smiling and breathless. I have a cab downstairs, he says. He puts his arm around my mother's shoulder to guide her and reaches down with his other hand to pick up the neatly packed suitcase waiting at the door.

Another scream. I could hear it through my humming, and it jolted me. Hands covering my face, I curled into myself, tucking the sheet tightly all around me. I was sure my mother was grabbing her sheet while she groaned. Maybe she had fallen off the bed and was lying on the floor. My mother shouted her boyfriend's name, but he wasn't there, so the midwife said that she was instead. My mother gripped her hand tightly, crushing it.

Her boyfriend is at the hospital. Dry scrubbed hands, smelling so clean. Green gown and a green shower cap. The doctor walks around the bed, eyebrows pushed together as he checks her pulse and reads the data sheets shooting out of a machine. A grin of anticipation is on her face. When the doctor tells her to push, she moans, but even the nurses who pass by her room can't hear her through the closed door.

The linen closet in our apartment opened, its squeak taking me away from the hospital. Iona must have been getting a towel to wipe my mother's forehead. There were too many voices coming from my mother's room, and I couldn't tell who they were. Iona came into our room, and I lay as still as possible. Standing below my bunk, she was watching me, I knew, and I wondered if she could see through the sheet with her glasses.

"I can't believe you aren't even getting up for this. I can't believe you're pretending to sleep through this," she said and closed the door.

Pressing myself against the wall and then into the mattress, I wanted to disappear. I tried to become the wall, unable to hear the grunts from a mother's throat as she lay in pain, reaching out to a stranger's hand.

We visit her the day after the birth. The three of us standing side by side, Iona and Miles and Casey, three siblings visiting their new sister or brother. A row of babies faces us, each one small and red and wrapped tightly in a cocoon of white cotton. Each one in its own miniature bed. I tap on the glass, whispering hello and welcome to the world. Iona laughs and says the baby wouldn't understand or hear me. Miles, bored after a while, drifts down the hall toward a window or a mysterious closed door.

My humming wouldn't stop the sounds. They only grew louder the more still I was, following me as I sank deeper into the mattress. My throat was almost completely closed, blocking a cough. I felt it explode inside of me instead. The thought of my mother lying helpless on her bed while that woman had come into her house kept me from running to help Iona. The memory of that woman and the fast and clear sound of her footsteps in the hall made me feel low and hollow.

My mother had been lying in her bed, all stomach, when that woman walked into her room. She had sunk deeper into her mattress just as she should have been jumping out of it. She had sniffled and opened a book to read just when she should have been storming through the apartment, grabbing her coat to chase the woman.

It was the thought of my mother hiding that kept me paralyzed. She had hidden while that woman, with her back tight and thorny as a long-stemmed rose, had stalked confidently out of the apartment.

The next morning we walked. Two sisters and a brother walking toward the train station, leaving their mother behind. Iona had waked me, holding clothes I had laid out the night before. I watched Iona dress and followed in the same order. Our stiff corduroy pants rubbed together as we moved, snapping in the grooves. My old shoes looked older in contrast to my crisp pants. I sweated in my velour shirt.

Iona walked ahead, leading us. She wouldn't look at me because I had stayed in bed the night before, and I felt ashamed. Last night she had remained awake, forcing herself to listen, waiting to see if she could be of any help. Miles sang softly under his breath, and the spring in his step made me wonder if he noticed Iona ignoring us. When we crossed Broadway, my sister slowed her pace to walk beside me and Miles, guiding us past the cars.

I walked alone into my classroom. Quietly, timidly, cautiously. No, nobody will notice me. But a woman with thin lips the same shade as her white skin walked right up. As she leaned down to ask who I was, I noticed that her eyebrows were painted on. A smell of thick paste and pencil shavings filled the room. The desks were lined up in perfect rows, each wiped clean and shining. Small wooden chairs stood at each desk, scarred by the carving of a name or the jabbing of a pencil.

"And who are you?" the teacher asked, and I wanted to lick my finger to rub out her eyebrows.

"Casey."

"And where is your mother?"

I looked around the room again. The other children in their stiff new clothes held their mother's hand, wrapped their arms around her leg, or pulled at her blouse. I pressed my back against the wall. I looked up confidently, right into her eyes so she would see I was telling the truth.

"My mother left already. She was in a hurry not to be late for work."

"I see," she said, and her lips tightened, almost completely disappearing.

She turned to the room and announced that class would begin. Mothers unhooked their children. Little hands were pulled off of waists, arms, legs. One girl slid down her mother's body and hugged her ankle. Her mother bent down and gently lifted her into a standing position. She brushed away the hair sticking to the girl's wet cheeks, kissed her on the head, whispered in her ear, and left the room.

I pictured Iona in her classroom on the floor above. Her glasses slowly moving down her nose. Her back straight, her arms folded. She probably had stacked her notebooks neatly inside the desk. I thought of Miles in the room next to Iona's, staring at the tree just outside the window, his desk shaking as he played the drums on his thigh. After a while he would pull out a book that he had brought from home and begin reading, hunched over so the teacher couldn't see.

A long chart of the alphabet stretched across the wall in my classroom, each letter wrapped up in an illustration. A snake twisting around an S or a zebra running through a Z. I looked up at my teacher. She leaned her head toward her right shoulder as she spoke, and I knew it would fall that way over a book she was holding up to read to the class.

*   *   *

My mother was still asleep after school, and I wondered if she had ever gotten up. Iona pushed me into her room so I could be there when she woke up. The new baby was also asleep. It was wrapped in a blanket and placed in a drawer that my mother had taken out of the bureau. I knew that the baby was out of my mother's stomach, but it still looked like something was inside because there was no way she could button her jeans yet. A pile of sheets she had used the night before lay on the floor, waiting for Iona to take away and wash.

The room was so quiet I could only sit at the foot of the bed, listening to my mother and the baby breathe. It smelled like someone else's room, slick and wet, the inside of a body. I looked at the floor. My mother had been on it the night before, making those loud noises.

The sun hit her bed. My mother changed in the light, her brown hair glowing red. And I remembered the days in Riverside Park as she sat in the sun on a bench while I played. I remembered the two of us lying in the grass, searching for four-leaf clovers. That's my mother, I would think. My perfectly stone-carved mother. Now, sitting on the floor with my eyes just over the top of the bed, I saw a leg, a bent arm, and a stream of red hair. A miniature brown hand moved in the drawer, and the baby made a noise. My mother turned. Her hazel eyes opened, glowing clear green. She yawned and raised her arm to stretch. Shifting again, she saw me.

"Oh, it's you," she said. "Just sitting there watching me." She reached out her hand to me. "Come on," she whispered. I was scared of her. I was scared of the smell, the sheets, the brown hand, and my mother's loose stomach, but I stood up and walked toward her as though my sister were still pushing me from behind. She pulled me close, folding her arms around me.

My throat cleared, air came in deeply, filling my lungs, and I felt my body grow stronger. A breeze blew through the half-open windows and the sheer white curtains became waves. My mother's bed was a raft and we were alone on it, her arms clasping me tightly so that I wouldn't fall, her face buried in the back of my neck, leaving a cool spot of water behind. I pushed myself closer to her and she curved around me. Another breeze blew, softer, filtered through the curtains, covering us both evenly.

My mother fell asleep, and I slid out of her grasp. In the kitchen, I opened the refrigerator and the cabinets, but they were all empty. Still hazy, I drifted down to Marisol and Jasmine's, grabbing a new book from school on my way. At the door, I heard her brothers again. Hungry, I waited like a hunter at the top of the stairs. After a while I opened my book, occasionally eyeing the door. But when the door did open, it was Marisol, carrying a bag of garbage. She glanced toward the stairs and stopped when she saw me.

"Hey, what are you doing up there?" she asked, pushing the garbage down the incinerator.

"I don't know," I answered, putting my face in my lap.

She called me to come down, and I followed her voice. The front door opened to sounds of a television, radio, and pool balls clicking. Safe in the kitchen, I watched Marisol begin dinner. She rubbed a chicken with butter, blending it into the skin. Handing me a bowl and a pile of carrots, she asked me to scrape them. She poured a glass of soda and placed it in front of me.

Marisol was singing softly, her back to me, when the brother walked in. "It's our little upstairs neighbor," he said, looking over Marisol's shoulder as she cooked. And then he turned to look at me, a grin on his face. His thumb hooked into his jeans pocket, one leg bent lower than the other, putting his shoulders off balance. His facial hair had grown, no longer prickly. He stared at me, and I wished I had never left my apartment. We would have found something to eat. Maybe my mother would have cooked.

He walked slowly toward the table, Marisol still facing the

counter. A wider grin. I scraped carrots intently. He bent down and put his lips to my ear so that his whisper came out as a scream.

"*Rubia!*"

It left my ear wet and itching. He stood up, and I felt him looking at the top of my head for a moment before he left the room. The carrots were finished, and I pushed the bowl to the other side of the table. Marisol poured detergent over her hands, washing the butter off. I felt for my pocket. My fingers slipped in between the covers of my book, running over the pages. I closed my eyes and lifted a hand to my nose, hoping to catch the smell of paper.

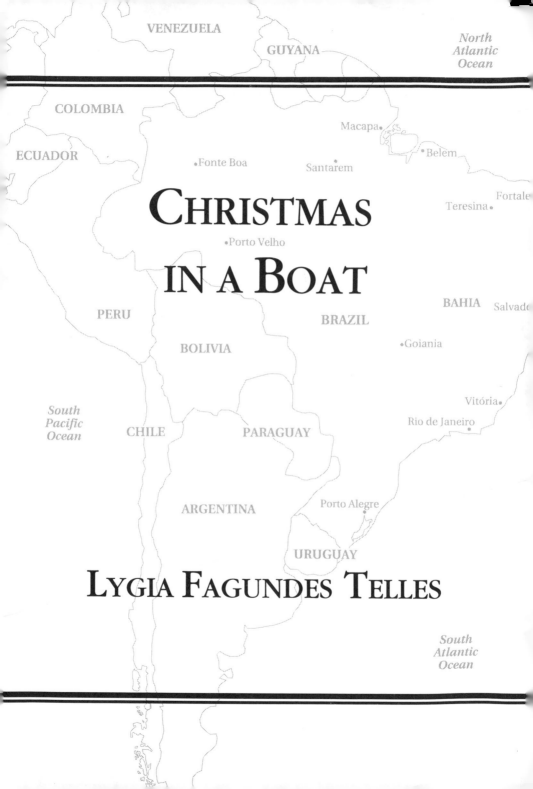

CHRISTMAS IN A BOAT

LYGIA FAGUNDES TELLES

Lygia Fagundes Telles was born and raised in São Paulo, Brazil. She holds a law degree from the University of São Paulo. Ms. Telles has written more than a dozen books, including several novels and many collections of short stories. A number of her books have been published abroad, including three in English: *The Marble Dance, The Girl in the Photograph,* and *Tigrela and Other Stories.* She has been awarded the most prestigious Brazilian literary awards, including the National Book Institute Award in 1958, the Coelho Neto Award from the Brazilian Academy of Letters in 1973, and the Pedro Nava Award for the Best Book of the Year in 1989.

Ms. Telles lives in São Paulo.

I prefer not to remember why I was on the boat. I just know that all around us everything was silence and darkness. In the vessel, rough and uncomfortable, only four passengers. A flickering lantern threw its light on us: an old man, a woman with her baby, and me.

The old man, a drunk in rags, had lain down on the bench and spoken gentle words to an invisible friend; now he was asleep. The woman was seated between us, clasping a swaddled child in her arms. She was young and pale. The long dark cloak covering her head made her seem an ancient figure.

As I had come aboard I had thought of speaking to her. But now we had to be nearing the end of the journey, and still I hadn't thought of anything to say.

Nor did it seem fitting to strike up a conversation in that boat, so Spartan, so stark. We were alone and it was best to do nothing, to say nothing, to barely glance at the black furrow that the boat was cutting into the river. I leaned over the worm-eaten wooden railing and lit a cigarette. Here we were, the three of us, like silent corpses sailing into the darkness in an ancient boat of the dead. Nonetheless, we were alive. And it was Christmas.

The box of matches slipped from my hand and almost fell into the water. I stooped down to pick it up. Feeling splashes on my face, I bent down further and dipped my fingertips in the water.

"How cold it is," I said, surprised, drying my hand.

"But in the morning it is hot."

I turned to the woman, who was cradling the child and watching me with a faint smile. I sat down next to her on the bench. She had beautiful clear eyes, extraordinarily brilliant. I noticed that her clothes, though threadbare, had character and bespoke dignity.

"In the mornings this river is hot," she repeated, looking straight at me.

"Hot?"

"Hot and green, so green that the first time I washed a pile of clothes in it I thought they would come out green. Is this your first time on the river?"

I looked away, down at the wide, worn planks. I answered her with a question:

"I take it you live near here?"

"In Lucena. I don't know how many times I have taken this boat, but I never expected to on a day like this . . ."

The child stirred and began to cry softly. The woman pressed it closer to her breast. She covered its head with her shawl and began lulling it with a tender rocking movement. Her hands fretted nervously over the shawl, but her face remained calm.

"Your son?"

"Yes. He's ill, I'm going to a specialist. The chemist in Lucena reckoned I should see a doctor right away. Until yesterday he was all right, but he got worse again. A fever, just a fever . . . but God will not abandon me."

"Is he your youngest?"

She abruptly lifted her head and held her pointed chin high, but her eyes had a mild expression.

"He is my only child. My first-born died last year. He had climbed a wall, playing at magic, when he suddenly shouted I'm going to fly! And he threw himself off. It wasn't a great fall, the wall wasn't high, but he fell with such force . . . he was just over four."

I flicked the cigarette in the direction of the river; the butt struck the railing and rolled back still burning onto the deck. I reached for it with the tip of my shoe and slowly crushed it. I quickly had to find a way to divert the conversation back to the child who was sick—but alive.

"And your baby, how old is he?"

"He's almost a year old," and, in a different tone, hanging

her head, "He was such a happy child. He had such a passion for magic. Of course, he could not do any tricks, but he was so delightful . . . his last bit of magic was perfect, I'm going to fly! he said, spreading out his arms, and off he went."

I stood up. I had wanted to be alone that night, without memories, without pity. But knots (human knots such as these) were threatening to entangle me. I had managed to avoid them until that moment. But now I could no longer fight my way out.

"Will your husband be waiting for you?"

"My husband left me."

I sat down and wanted to laugh. Incredible. It had been sheer stupidity to ask the first question, and now I could no longer stop—oh, this system of communicating vessels.

"Has it been a long time? Since your husband . . ."

"It's been about six months. We lived so well together, so well. It happened when he ran into his old girlfriend. He had told me about it jokingly, Bila had grown ugly, of the two of them it was he who had kept his looks. . . . He did not mention her again. One morning he got up like every other morning, drank his coffee, read his newspaper, played with the baby, and went to work. And before leaving he lifted his hand like this. I was in the kitchen washing up, and he bid me farewell through the wire screen of the door. I remember I wanted to open the door—I don't like seeing anyone speak to me through the screen—but my hands were wet. Late that afternoon I received a card, he had sent me a card. I went to live with my mother in a house that we rented near my school. I'm a teacher."

I looked at the raging clouds flowing in the same direction as the river. Incredible. She was reciting this succession of disasters with such calm, with the voice of someone describing circumstances that had nothing to do with her. The poverty evident in the patching of her clothes was not enough; she had to lose her child, her husband, and now a shadow had come over the second child she was cradling in her arms. And there she was confiding in me without the slightest sign of bitterness. Impervious. Was this indifference? No, those fiery eyes were not capable of indifference. Nor those vigorous hands. Thoughtlessness? A dark irritation drove me on.

"Are you resigned?"

"I have my faith. God will not abandon me."

"God," I repeated vaguely.

"Don't you believe in God?"

"I believe in Him," I murmured. And hearing the feebleness of my answer, without knowing why, I became anxious. Now I understood. This was the secret behind her confidence, her calm. It was the kind of faith that could move mountains . . .

She lifted her child, shifting him from her right shoulder to her left. And she continued in a voice hot with passion:

"It was just after the death of my child. I woke up one night so desperate that I ran out into the street, I put on a coat and went out barefoot, crying, totally out of my mind, calling out to him . . . I sat on a bench in the park where he played every afternoon. And I pleaded, I pleaded with such force, that he who was so in love with magic would use this magic to appear to me just one more time, he didn't have to stay, just appear for an instant, just one more time, just once! When my tears dried, I laid my head on the bench and I don't know how but I fell asleep. Then I dreamt and in my dream God appeared, that is to say, I felt that He clasped my hand with His hand of light. And I saw my little boy playing in the Garden of Eden with little boy Jesus. The moment he saw me, he stopped playing and ran to me, laughing and kissing me so much, so much . . . he was so happy that I woke up laughing with the sun beating down on me."

I did not know what to say. I attempted a gesture. Then, just to do something, I lifted the corner of the shawl that covered the baby's head. I let the shawl drop and stared down at the deck. The child was dead. The mother continued rocking him, pressing him against her chest. But he was dead.

I leaned on the railing of the boat and breathed hard: It was as if I were immersed to the neck in that water. I felt the woman move behind me.

"We're almost there," she announced.

I quickly picked up my bag. What was important now was to get away, to escape before she found out, to run from this horror. The boat was slowing, making a wide turn before docking. The ticket collector appeared and started shaking the old man who was sleeping:

"We're almost there! . . . Hey, we're almost there!"

I approached her, looking away.

"I think it best we say good-bye here," I said, bewildered, stretching my hand out to her.

She seemed not to notice it. She got up and turned as if to pick up her sack. I tried to help her, but instead of taking the sack that I held out to her—before I could stop her—she removed the shawl from the child's head.

"The little sleepyhead has waked up! And look at that, it seems the fever's gone too."

"He's awake?"

She smiled.

"Look!"

I bent over. The baby opened his eyes—those eyes that I had seen as so definitively shut. And he yawned, rubbing a little hand on his rosy cheek. I stared, dumbstruck.

"Well, Merry Christmas!" she said, slipping the sack onto her arm.

From under the black cloak with its crossed ends pulled back, her face shone. I squeezed her energetic hand and followed her with my eyes until she disappeared into the night.

Led by the ticket collector, the old man passed by,

resuming his tender conversation with the invisible friend.
I was the last to leave the boat. I turned back twice to look
at the river. And I could imagine how it would be in the
early morning: green and hot, green and hot.

Translated from the Portuguese
by Peter Constantine

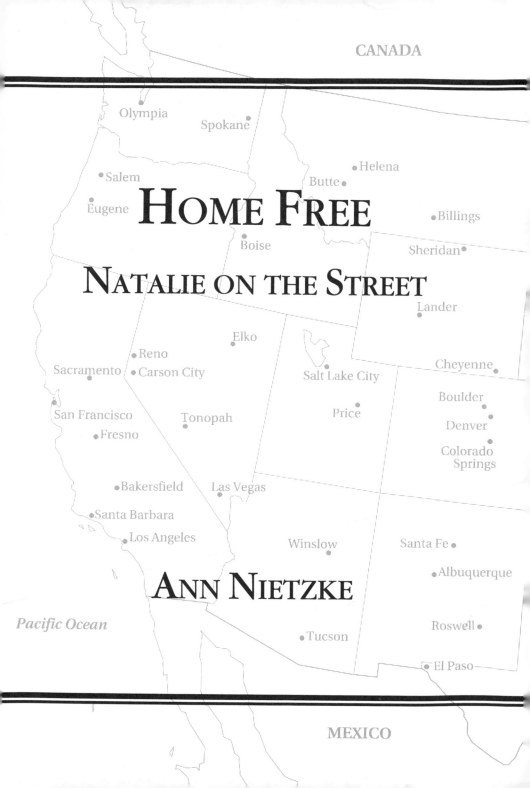

CANADA

HOME FREE

NATALIE ON THE STREET

ANN NIETZKE

Pacific Ocean

MEXICO

Ann Nietzke was born in Alton, Illinois. She holds a Bachelor of Science degree in English Education from the University of Illinois at Urbana and a Master's degree in English from Illinois State University. Ms. Nietzke has been an English instructor, medical transcriber, receptionist, and editorial consultant and was, for several years, a contributing editor to *Human Behavior* magazine. Since 1986, Ms. Nietzke has worked half time in a residential psychiatric program for people who are homeless and mentally ill.

Ms. Nietzke is the author of *Windowlight*, for which she received the 1982 Los Angeles PEN Award for Best First Fiction. In 1987 she was awarded a Creative Writing Fellowship by the National Endowment for the Arts, and in 1993 held a residency at the Macdowell Colony. Ms. Nietzke's short stories have appeared in magazines such as *Shenandoah*, *Other Voices*, and the *Massachusetts Review*. Her non-fiction articles have appeared in publications including *Cosmopolitan*, *Village Voice*, and *The Sun*.

Ms. Nietzke lives in Los Angeles. The following selection is an excerpt from her forthcoming book, *Natalie on the Street*, to be published by CALYX Books in the fall.

There is no simple way, no easy or uncomplicated way, to look into the face of a filthy old woman on the street. We are frightened or saddened or repelled, feel guilty if not resentful, and then we avert our eyes. In a society that disdains old women even in the best of circumstances, we are naturally overwhelmed by those who belong to no person or place, those who in the very state of their existence violate every conventional notion of "femininity" and force us to remember death. If the old gal is crazy as well—and it seems so many of them are—we're likely to hurry past, cross the street, avoid her altogether.

When Natalie first appeared in my neighborhood with her shopping cart and her miscellany of plastic bags, she drew particular attention, not because "bag ladies" are an uncommon sight in central Los Angeles, but because she chose to navigate the sidewalks of our narrow residential streets rather than sticking to Vermont or Western Avenue, Santa Monica or Olympic Boulevard. Jogging past her on my daily morning route, I would take to the gutter, relinquishing the entire walkway to Natalie as she inched her cart along. If she looked my way at all it was with anger and suspicion, but I greeted her consistently with a neighborly "Good morning."

"*Hah!*" she called back one day, her arm shooting straight up and out to wave me on with a vengeance.

Having spent much of my adolescence in small-town Mississippi, I am often still impelled to "say hey" to strangers: At 7 a.m. I will greet any female I meet and any male who lacks an overtly menacing aura. There is no doubt, too, that my part-time clerical job in a psychiatric shelter for homeless people has deepened my tolerance for unusual behavior and broadened my perspective on who looks or does not look threatening. So I would always call out "Good morning" to Natalie, until occasionally she would give me a stiff, childlike wave (from the elbow down), not smiling, demanding loudly of the space between us, "What's *her* hurry-hurry-hurry?"

Even my lazy pace must have seemed rapid to her, pushing a resistant cart stuffed with clothing and bedding, piled high with paper and plastic bags themselves overloaded with who knew what. She would shove the cart a few feet and then have to retrace her steps for the four or five auxiliary bags behind her, set them carefully down again, and give the cart another push. Progress was slow, without apparent destination, and the technique, which seemed to require her full concentration, was obviously tedious and exhausting. As the weeks went by I noticed Natalie standing wearily for longer and longer periods between locomotions, though she would keep her hands on the red handlebar of the cart as if at any second she might move on.

"That's what that officer told me," she whispered to me later. "Keep moving, see. As soon as I quit moving is right when the trouble starts."

For most Americans the word *homeless* has become common enough to have lost both its shock value and its power to stir us. It is one of those adjectives that have crossed over to categorical noun: the blind, the deaf, the mentally ill, the disabled, the poor, the elderly, the homeless. But to endure homelessness for any extended period of time and still maintain integrity of the self requires more "sanity" than many of us possess; those who are less tightly wrapped to begin with can be easily undone by the streets. To lack a home is to lack, most basically, shelter from the elements. But that lack of shelter also means no toilet facilities, no place to cook food, no place to bathe or wash hair or change clothes, no place to store belongings. We say *home* is where we live, as if we cannot *live* without one. "At home" we can be at ease and comfortable ("Make yourself at home.").

Our *residence* is where we *reside* (from the Latin "to sit back" or "remain sitting"). Having an *abode* is what enables us to *abide*—to bear the difficulties and sufferings of life, to tolerate and endure and restore ourselves to the world. Lacking a home, we lack protection from the wickedness of strangers, we lack the dignity of belonging somewhere, we lack the privilege of determining who is welcome to be near us and who is not. We lack, finally, the identity that comes with having an address, which in some deep way serves to register formally our presence on earth.

No dwelling place for Natalie meant no place to "stay," implying her constant mobility. While for most of us "moving" means changing abodes, for Natalie it just meant keeping out of everyone's way. Her shopping cart functioned simultaneously as luggage, van, closet, cabinet, and furniture in what had become her traveling *apartment*, which she used to set herself *apart* from her environment on the street, where her personal boundaries came to include not just her person but her cart and bags as well. One could never deal with Natalie alone; one had to deal with Natalie and the cart and *all* her bags, whose number varied daily, mostly upward. Despite her lifetime of debilitating schizophrenic illness, Natalie perceived her need for a home, and her ability to improvise one for herself represented to me a core of sanity within her that refused to budge. Though the cart was full of clothing she never wore and bedding she never used, and the bags held mostly waste paper, rotting food, garbage, and feces, these possessions enabled Natalie to claim space as her own wherever she went and thereby maintain a sense of dignity and pride (telling me more than once that she knew people were jealous of her things, which sometimes caused her to feel sorry for them).

"What have you been doing today, honey?" she asked me one day after we had become friends.

"Not much," I said. "Mostly just cleaning my apartment."

"This place needs straightening, too," Natalie said, in perfectly normal woman-talk. "I need to reorganize everything." She surveyed her belongings, grouped along the sidewalk near her cart, with the critical eye of any decent housekeeper. "I need some more bags, is what I need. But I just don't seem to have the time. Every day around here is busier than the last one."

I suppose if Natalie had been able to keep on the move as instructed I might never have gotten involved with her. But looking out my window early one October morning, I realized that she was still lying flat on the sidewalk beside her cart, that in fact it had been several days since I'd noticed her sitting up, much less standing in her usual manner. Dread gathered at the pit of my stomach, dread that she might be injured or sick or even dead, and that I was going to be the one to find out which it was.

"She's moved," I told myself. "She's probably moved a dozen times and ended up back here to sleep." But on my way out to work I stopped at my next-door neighbor's. "Have you seen that woman across the street up and around the past few days?"

"Who?" Joyce said. "The bag lady? I think she's been over there all week long."

Crossing kitty-corner, I braced myself. This approach felt very different from running past her incidentally. If she were sick she might not appreciate being disturbed. A madwoman, after all, is often an angry woman—I had more than once heard Natalie loudly scolding real or invisible passersby. I stopped in the street eight or ten feet from where she lay covered head-to-toe with what looked like a black garbage bag over a dirty, thin white cotton sheet. The strip of grass between her and the curb still held its share of dew, but maybe the plastic had kept her dry.

"Lady?" I called out. "Excuse me, lady. Hey, lady?"

She sat straight up with an almost violent suddenness, apparently startled from sleep. She gazed at me with a kind of blank and groggy sweetness instead of the usual suspicion.

"I'm sorry," I said. "Are you all right? Are you sick?"

"No," Natalie said softly, "I just haven't combed my hair yet. They tell me to comb that hair in the morning. You know." Her pale, blondish-gray hair hung straight from beneath the tight, light blue knit cap she always wore, not quite shoulder length but getting there. What looked like a wig in a small paper bag she kept in her cart turned out to be her own hair, salvaged from these vigorous daily combings.

"So you're not sick, then," I said. "I hadn't seen you move for so long I was afraid something was wrong."

"Resting," she said. "I have to rest for the weary, don't I? They don't want me to wear myself down."

"So you can still walk all right?"

"Sure," she whispered confidentially. "This one and that one and the other one. You know."

"Well, do you have food and water? Do you have everything you need?" Natalie ignored the stupidity of this question and said, "Oh yes," with conviction.

"Everything I need is here. Except I have to find that comb."

I figured Natalie to be in her late sixties, but then, when I thought about it, I subtracted a few years to compensate for the way her illness and life on the streets must have weathered her. It was shocking to learn later that she was seventy-four years old, though as soon as I heard it I realized that she looked every bit of seventy-four and more—in voice, in manner, and in the slow, cautious way she would shuffle along when no one was pressuring her. Something in me had needed to keep her under seventy, as if that were the bitter, arbitrary age past which the idea of homelessness became unbearable to contemplate.

Gradually I began to suspect that she must have recently been released from a hospital or nursing facility, if not a board-and-care home, and one day I glimpsed a plastic name band on her wrist, though I was unable to read it. "They tell me not to show that, honey," she whispered when I asked, and the next time I looked it was gone. Natalie's clothing appeared to have been chosen carefully with regard to both color and practicality for the street. She wore a very heavy, long wool skirt, dark blue with a diagonal stripe of burgundy, and her dark blue nylon car-coat, a zip-up model with several pockets, matched it perfectly. Only her shoes seemed insubstantial—plain black flats with nylons instead of something sturdy and warm with socks. The blue knit hat complemented her eyes, and then there was the final touch—white nylon church gloves with all the fingertips cut off. The left fourth finger was slit vertically as well, just enough to reveal a plain silver ring containing a small, highly polished, dark blue marbled stone. The clothes were hardly fresh, but neither were they soiled and smelly. The skirt, though several clothespins were necessary to hold it up, was superior to pants because it kept her covered as she squatted to urinate and defecate. The jacket pockets, inside and out, held Natalie's most personal belongings (such as comb and makeup) and served in place of a purse. I kept wondering if Natalie had managed to set herself up so skillfully or whether some-one hadn't helped prepare her for life on the street (or *back* on the street), but questions designed to get at her "story" only inspired her to bizarre combinations of memory and fantasy.

"Clark Gable, oh yes, he's a friend of mine. And of course Sammy Davis, Jr., was there, too. They tell me to let my hair grow longer now. That was on the corner down there on Third Street where they had that fireworks celebration. They keep track of it all in Sacramento."

"Well, are you a Californian, then?" I asked.

"He told me. I mean. I'm not supposed to say, but he said you can't help it, that's what you are, you're a CALIFORNIAN!!! Shhhh. There's no need for everybody to hear everything."

"Do you like to take a drink once in a while?" I asked, wondering if she might have just been through detox.

"Oh, no, no, honey," she whispered. "I don't even smoke a cigarette. I used to take a drink once in a while, but I have to be careful now." She looked around as if someone were eavesdropping. "You know."

"It's true," I said. "You do have to be careful out here. Do you ever hear voices speaking to you? You know what I mean? Voices?"

"No, I don't hear any voices, honey." She was answering very much in earnest, though what she said was plainly untrue. "I have trouble with people disappearing, though. I'll look up and they'll be gone. Just like that. Boy-o-boy-o-boy. What would you make of that?"

"Aren't you afraid out here?" I asked. "Won't you let me take you to a shelter where you can at least sleep indoors at night?"

"I'm better off in the open air," she insisted. "They gave me lye in there, you know. Put it all the way down my throat." She rubbed her throat as if it were sore.

"Well, aren't you afraid after dark out here?"

"I'm not afraid of the dark. Are you afraid of the dark, honey? So many people are, I know. I used to get those shots for $9. Then they gave me the lye. And I used to be able to wash at that faucet behind the drugstore. Over here on Vermont. But the emperor tells me not to wash too much now, anyway. It's the Negroes, honey. They're trying to stay young at our expense. Believe me. But as far as a Californian, they've got all the necessary information in Sacramento, so it doesn't matter wherever I go or not. This and that and the other thing. You know." She'd wink her conspiratorial wink.

"Yeah," I'd say. "I know."

When I returned home the day I first went to check on Natalie, she had managed to relocate her cart and bags about thirty or forty feet west of the corner where she'd been camping all that week. She may have taken my approach as a subtle hint to move on rather than genuine concern, but whatever the motivation, it was extremely fortunate, since she would probably not have survived the night in her previous spot. Not long after midnight I was awakened by a thunderous crash, accompanied by a loud rush of water. A car had apparently run the stop sign beneath my window, then jumped the opposite curb, tearing a fire hydrant from its moorings and crashing into a palm tree before coming to rest on the very section of sidewalk where Natalie had lain so long. No one in the car seemed to be hurt, but the pavement was soon flooded, water gushing down the gentle incline in front of my apartment building with all the resonance of a mountain creek. Two police cars, a firetruck, a water department van all arrived in turn with flashing lights. Whenever incidental headlights approached the corner, I could see Natalie up the street, standing at the ready behind her cart, facing away from all the commotion, conspicuously minding her own business.

No arrest was made, though I found it hard to believe a sober driver could have accomplished such an accident. Eventually the police and fire department pulled away, leaving the D.W.P. man to maneuver beneath the car with his various tools until he found the magic connection that subdued the flow to a trickle. Then the three young men—boys, really—spent several minutes assaying the damage to their car. There was some discussion whether they'd be able to back up over the hydrant without making things worse, but finally, with much grinding and scraping, they did get the car off the curb and into the intersection, where the motor died and refused to revive, oblivious to their curses both in Spanish and English. They pushed the car on down the street then and left it parked alongside Natalie, who scurried out of headlight range and hid behind her cart as the boys walked off into the damp autumn night.

Coming back from my run late the next morning, I stopped to say hello to Natalie, who was up, alert, sitting on the sidewalk behind her cart with a blanket over her legs.

"A lot of excitement last night, huh?" I said. "I'm so glad you moved away from that corner."

"They say it's best to keep moving." She spoke with a tone of pride in having done the right thing.

"No, I mean I think that car might have hit you if you'd stayed where you were," I said.

"You never know what they'll do," she said firmly, not whispering. "They'll beat you to a bloody pulp."

"I mean the car that hit the fire hydrant," I said. "Did you hear all that water?"

"An uncle of mine was a fireman. Get all these babies and throw them down, you know? To save them? Burn 'em to a crisp if you didn't."

Obviously I was much more impressed by her brush with death than Natalie herself, whose world seemed such a relentlessly dangerous place that she could take a great deal in stride.

"How about a cup of coffee?" I said. "Can I bring you a cup of coffee?"

Natalie reached quickly down into her nearest bag and pulled out the broken-off head of a hammer. "This is what I used to pry open that closet when I was nine years old," she said, holding it out for me to inspect. I didn't want to ask about the closet, real or delusional.

"I'm going to have some coffee," I said. "Can I bring you some?"

"Can't you give a man a little pleasure? Can't you give a man a little pleasure? That's all he would ever say." She sat silent for a moment, then looked at me directly. "I believe you've got some gray in your hair."

"Yes, I do," I said. "My hair started getting gray when I was twenty-eight years old."

"Well, mine started getting gray when I was nine years old." She laughed to let me know this was a joke, so I laughed with her.

"Have you got a cup I can use?" I asked. "I don't have any throwaway cups."

"They'll give you one," Natalie said. "Go over there to the donut house."

"No," I said. "I'm bringing it from home. From where I live. Do you like cream and sugar?"

"Don't put anything in it to make me sleep. I don't have any trouble sleeping."

"You want cream?" I asked again.

"Not if it's gonna put me to sleep. I don't know why, but they always put something in it to knock me out."

"I'm not going to do that," I said. "I would never do that. I'm going to put some lowfat milk in it and some sugar. That's all. Do you have a cup I can use?"

Natalie began reaching for various plastic bags and rustling through their contents with some thoroughness. To me they all appeared the same, most filled with more plastic or with paper plates and trash and wads of paper, others stuffed with ratty-looking bits of cloth. Eventually she pulled out a sixteen-ounce styrofoam cup from Winchell's Donuts, reasonably clean, with its lid still attached. She started to hand it to me, then jerked it back and removed the lid to peer inside. "Well," she said, holding it out for me to look, "that's what came out of me." Inside were two solid, well-formed turds. "I hate to have to show that to you, honey," she whispered solemnly. "But there it is."

"There it is," I said. "I hate you had to, too." The urge to laugh was overcoming my disgust. "I'll just bring you a cup of mine and get it back later. Please. Don't search anymore." Natalie shrugged her shoulders and replaced the lid on the cup, which she then stuck back deep into its bag.

As I approached a few minutes later with the coffee, Natalie was on her feet, leaning against the cart and holding her side as if in pain. At the curb ahead of her the boys from last night had returned to work on their car. Natalie was grumbling to herself, and it soon became apparent that there had been a less than friendly exchange. I heard her mutter something about "sonsabitches," and the oldest boy, the driver, stepped from behind the raised hood to point at Natalie with pliers.

"If you don't like it here, go somewhere else," he said. "Nobody says you have to stand beside us. Take your garbage and go. Bag lady."

"Yeah," his younger and smaller companion chimed in. "Old bag lady. Why don't you go somewhere else? Old bag." All three of them laughed in the loud and easy way some Latinos seem to cultivate for outdoors.

I stopped in my tracks and stood glaring at them until they shut up and resumed business with the car. They had fallen from my good graces when they crashed into my sleep, and now I could feel blood pounding in my neck because I wasn't telling them off on Natalie's behalf as well as my own.

"They'll tear up everything you've got," she warned me as she sipped, ignoring my question about why she was clutching the side of her abdomen. "Watch your back every minute, I mean it. Somebody like you can't imagine the meanness that goes on in this world. What on earth did you put in there? It tastes awfully good."

"Milk and sugar," I said. "Coffee and water and sugar and milk."

It is perhaps remarkable that adolescent name-calling was the only overt and deliberate cruelty I witnessed toward Natalie her whole time in the neighborhood. Eventually a number of women, in particular, went out of their way to be kind, partly no doubt from "motherly instinct" (it is always "women's work" to feed and clothe and cleanse the helpless). But in addition I think many women, especially unmarried women, have at least considered the fact that we live only a step or two or three from the streets ourselves and that, in America, the older we get the more precarious our position becomes. With two words, *old bag*, a boy had reduced Natalie to an object of no more value than the thin sheets of plastic she used to organize and convey her life. Old bags. Old, dried-up breasts. Women past childbearing age, even proper, clean, sane ones, simply ain't worth what they used to be.

The autumn of the year Natalie appeared seemed to me cooler and windier and rainier than usual, though I may have just been more conscious of the nuances of weather because I was so keenly aware of her enduring it all unsheltered. For a time she parked her cart at the very far end of my block, directly on the corner itself where there was no tree to lean against, no shade, no structure of any kind to offer even minimal privacy or cover. I had to press my face sideways against my window screen to keep track of her there, and one afternoon when a chilly rain began to fall I saw her kneeling beside the cart completely unprotected. By the time I dug up a thin blue plastic picnic cloth from the bottom of the drawer and got to her with it, someone else had already contributed a large sheet of sturdy, clear plastic, which Natalie was busy spreading over the cart and attendant bags rather than over herself.

"You better get under there," I told her. "It's raining harder all the time. Take this, too."

She took the tablecloth and stood with it folded tight in both hands against her chest, as if I'd presented her a ceremonial flag.

"I wouldn't want to get this wet," she said. "It's so beautiful. Are you sure you don't need it?"

"Use it," I said. "Please. Put it over your head and shoulders before you get soaked." I was standing there with no umbrella myself.

"Oh, I'll dry out," Natalie reassured me. "He doesn't like me to be too dry, you know. And if you get him mad, then you've got trouble, so I'd about as soon not. You see what I'm saying."

"I see what you're saying," I said. "But let's just unfold the thing and put it around your shoulders, at least." I reached for the plastic.

"Well, if you want it back you can have it," she said, not, however, offering it. "You look like you're getting wet, honey. You've got the prettiest hands." We admired my hands for a while.

"I've got some gloves you can have," I told her. "Yours look a little breezy."

Natalie examined her protruding fingertips and laughed. "Oh, he likes me to wear these," she said pleasantly. "I don't know why." She spread the vertical tear on her ring finger to expose the polished stone for me.

"It's pretty," I said. "That's clever how you can show it off that way."

"Yes," Natalie said. "It's what you might call a basic heirloom, I guess. The whole arrangement."

"Have you had anything to eat today?" I asked her. I had brought her coffee several times but never food. Food felt like too much involvement, too much responsibility—that terrible common-sense admonition not to feed strays. "What have you had to eat today?"

"Nothing yet today," Natalie said. "I've got crackers a lady brought. Would you care for a cracker?" She began to rummage among the sheltered bags.

"No," I said quickly. "No, thanks, I've eaten. What if I

boiled you some eggs? Do you like boiled eggs?"

Her eyes lit up. "Oh, boy," she said. "I used to have them. I haven't had them anymore. But I don't want to run my bill up too high, you know."

"Don't worry about it," I said. "I'll be back."

I took her three hard-boiled eggs in a paper towel, along with a pink-and-gray knit hat and glove set, still in its gold display box from several Christmases ago. Natalie was lying flat on the sidewalk, head and all beneath the heavy clear plastic with her bags, still clutching the folded square of picnic cloth I'd brought.

"Eat them while they're warm," I told her. "They'll feel good in your tummy."

"Yes, I need to settle that stomach. I don't know what's the matter with it." She sat up on one elbow and took the eggs, though she was much more enthusiastic about the gold box than about the food or the new accessories. "You don't want to give that up," she said, quickly shoving it in amid her damp and airless aromatic sacks. "It almost looks like the gift of the Magi, doesn't it?"

"Peel the eggs," I said, backing away. "Eat them now, before they get cold."

"Boy, they'll be good, too," she said, making no move. "Thank you ever so much."

"I can drive you to a shelter anytime," I said. "All you have to do is say the word."

"No, I'm already home free now, honey," she said. "Do I owe you anything for the eggs? They tell me not to run my bill way up."

Later that afternoon the rain slacked off, and I could see Natalie sitting up on her knees again, shaking out the blue plastic and then carefully refolding it to store away. She had replaced her blue knit cap with the pink and gray one, which I took as a good sign, since the new one was thicker and warmer. Next morning, though, I noticed the blue cap was back—the hat-and-glove ensemble, sans gold box, had taken its place among a wad of miscellaneous clothing in one corner of her cart and remained exactly there, I think, for as long as Natalie remained in the neighborhood.

Within a few days, something or someone caused her to break camp suddenly and move back to the corner directly opposite my building. She stood there poised with her cart in the mid-morning sun, shouting long enough and loud enough to penetrate through closed windows and into the farthest side of my apartment, though except for scattered obscenities I couldn't make out her words. I boiled some eggs and went out to see what the fuss was about.

"You get away from here, by God." I wasn't sure if she was talking to me because her eyes had a vacant, glazed look, and her head had not yet turned my way. I stopped in the middle of the street, though, ten or twelve feet away from her.

"Are you mad this morning, Natalie?" I asked. "I could hear you all the way upstairs. It sounds like you're angry at someone." She turned to face me and directed her full force of fury in my direction.

"You'd be mad, too, if somebody put a bomb in your cart and tried to blow your damn cart away."

"Oh," I said, more calmly than I felt. Her cart didn't appear in the least disturbed since the last time I'd seen it.

"And if they tried to talk when you don't feel like having a conversation." She stretched her neck and yelled this somewhere to the left and over my head, but I still felt it was aimed at me. I had a feeling neighbors were peeping out their windows to see what I was doing to make the shouting worse.

"So do you want some eggs?" I held them out for her to see.

"Yes, I do." She responded quietly in a rational tone of voice. I approached her quickly, handed them over, and retreated without hesitation.

"Thank you very much," she said, formal and polite.

"You're very welcome," I said. The storm, whatever it was, appeared to have subsided. Natalie arranged her bags at the base of the palm tree, spread out the furry black lining of an old coat on the sidewalk, and settled down for a stay of indefinite duration.

From that point on, by virtue of her proximity if nothing else, Natalie took up a unique kind of daily residence in my thoughts—I could no longer buy groceries, cook, discard leftovers, or deal with sacks, bags, or containers of any kind without some consideration of Natalie.

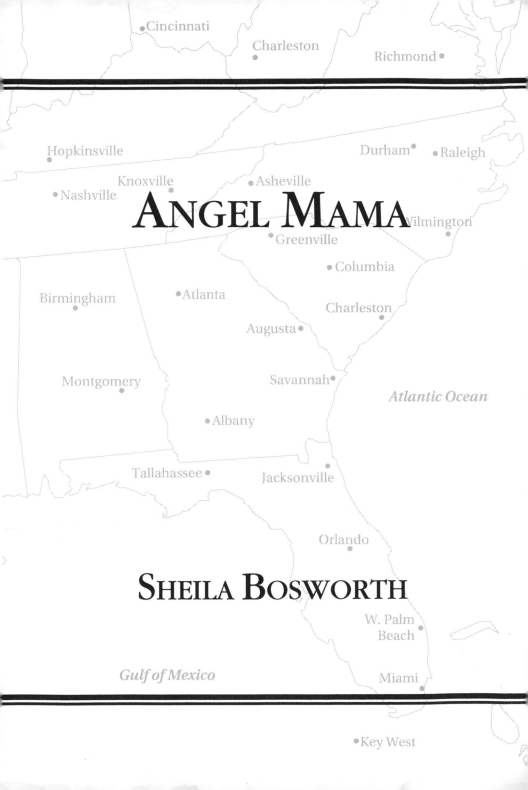

ANGEL MAMA

SHEILA BOSWORTH

Sheila Bosworth was born in New Orleans, Louisiana. She attended Tulane University, where she completed a double major in French and English. Ms. Bosworth is the author of two novels, *Almost Innocent* and *Slow Poison*.

The following selection is a one-woman play that was first performed in 1993 by Carol Sutton as part of "Native Tongues." An evening of monologues about life in New Orleans, "Native Tongues" was produced by All Kinds of Theatre and directed by Carl Walker.

Ms. Bosworth lives in Covington, Louisiana, with her husband and two daughters. She is currently at work on her new novel, *Ransom the Captive*.

Aɴɢᴇ̀ʟᴇ *is an African-American woman. She lives in two rooms with a balcony above a tavern on Frenchmen Street, in the Faubourg Marigny on the edge of the New Orleans Vieux Carré. For the past week, she's been too sick to cook or leave her rooms.*

This is a relatively good day for ᴀɴɢᴇ̀ʟᴇ, *she's feeling a little better than she did yesterday. She has dressed in a rather shabby red satin robe, which hangs on her bony frame, and she has caught back her hair with a rhinestone clip. On her feet she wears faded red satin mules. Though her face shows signs of illness, she has on rouge and bright red lipstick.*

ᴀɴɢᴇ̀ʟᴇ *half-reclines on an iron glider with threadbare cushions; the glider is positioned at an angle on an iron-railinged balcony outside her bedroom door, above the tavern. A rocking chair, a plastic dog on wheels, and a cardboard dollhouse can be seen in a corner of the balcony. Blues piano from the tavern downstairs is heard. The music fades as* ᴀɴɢᴇ̀ʟᴇ *begins to speak.*

It is the New Orleans carnival season, in winter of the present year. It is late afternoon. The lighting changes gradually from the colors of sunset to twilight gray to black.

ANGÈLE :

Speaking to the audience.

What's the worst thing you ever done, honey? Not counting sitting here with me. No, now don't tell me that visiting with Angèle the unemployed hooker isn't pretty low down on your badness list. Earlier this evening, I had a real high-class caller. One of them volunteers from that Catholic bunch calls themselves the

Lazarus House*? Now, what can that volunteer have done in her white-lady life that's so bad she got to punish herself with coming to see me? The woman was a wreck! Bet she had some Dr. Tichenor's antiseptic in her pocketbook, pair of rubber gloves stuff down in her brassiere, in case the diarear hit her while she's here and she have to touch my toilet. I hope that sweet darling brought her own toilet paper, too, because Lord knows what's crawling on mine.

She runs her hand shakily over her face, her neck, and then leans forward toward the audience.

Tell the truth: How bad I look? Used to be I couldn't sit out here two minutes this time of evening without mens hollering up at me. Holler, "Where the stairs at, sweet angel mama? Show me how I can climb up your stairway to heaven." Nobody hollering nothing now. Not since the virus come to call. Curtis be by in a minute, going to bring me a plate of beans and rice for my supper. Curtis my pimp. Was my pimp. Care to eat some supper with me and Curtis? I asked the volunteer woman to stay, but she said she had already ate. Uh-huh. I kind of figured she had. She looked like she could of *used* something to eat, little bit of a lady, sat down in that rocking chair and her feets barely scrape the floor. That rocker got its seat too high off the ground. Old wino carpenter over Burgundy Street hammered it together for me when my baby was born. She and me like to kill ourself more than once in that thing, get to rocking good and fly off it, land on our butt laughin.

She coughs slightly.

This volunteer wasn't no little girl, though. Had on a

* Lazarus House—AIDS hospice in New Orleans.

serious diamond ring. Her husband must be a funeral director, was what I thought, but it turn out he with the New Orleans city government. She have my sympathy, poor woman. And I could look in her big blue eyes and see I had hers. You might say *she* the funeral director. Well, she's free to direct mine.

She coughs violently.

Volunteers always be asking do I *need* anything. Truth be told, I wouldn't mind some liver. Not the kind with onions and gravy; I mean some *liver.* I need me a transplant. I seen on TV where they putting baboon livers in people. Doctor over at Charity say they won't give me one, though. Say the AIDS just going to wreck the baboon liver, too, so why waste one by puttin it in me? He can keep it. I ain't begging for no baboon liver. I been begging baboons for one thing or another all my life.

While I'm on the subject of begging, guess who that volunteer organization named itself after? A beggar in the bible! Lazarus. Jesus told a story about him. Old pain-in-the-butt Lazarus, always be rolling on the rug under the rich man table, talking 'bout, "Throw me down some roast beef! Let me have a handful of whatever you got that's good!" Look like the dinner party be asking, "Who let *him* in again? Boot Lazarus black self out of here!" What you want to bet Lazarus was a black man? I believe the rich people *did* hand Lazarus a bag full of breadcrumbs before they shove him down the steps, though. Pitiful old Lazarus . . . You know, I'm maybe talking about the wrong Lazarus here. That organization might be named for that other Lazarus, the one whose two sisters begged Jesus to raise him up after he had already died? Jesus did it, too. Must have had a softness in his heart for those sisters, because Jesus didn't go in much for trucking with corpses. Only one other corpse he raised up, to my knowledge, and that one was a rich man's little girl. Jesus say to the rich man, "Your little girl ain't dead, daddy! She just sleeping! Let me see can I wake her up." And he did, sure enough.

Some people act surprised I'm so familiar with my Bible. Well, listen, I was baptized Catholic, made my First Communion when I was seven years old, at Our Lady of Guadalupe, over on Rampart Street. Anyway, what do it matter which Lazarus those volunteer people calling themself after? Neither one turn me on. I bet Jesus rather eat his supper with a prostitute than with either one of them Lazaruses, the mean beggar *or* the damn mummy. Prostitute don't roll on no rich man carpet for crumbs, and I ain't never known a whore yet would ask to come back from the dead and live in this world a second time.

She begins to cough and tremble. She reaches for her shawl and wraps it around her thin shoulders.

What's the worst thing you ever done . . . I would've liked to heard that volunteer woman answer *that* question. Ten to one she'd have said something sexual. Picture that, if you can stand to: little white girl with that New Orleans city government worker.

She coughs violently and draws the shawl tighter around her shoulders. During the next speech—"Breeze . . . done"—she lights a half-dozen red-glassed votive candles on the balcony's iron railing ledge.

Breeze picking up . . . what I want to do now is to tell you the worst thing I ever done. Because . . . I'm scared to go to the priest in confession with it. I don't want to tell my business to no holy man. Ain't it a shame the Pope too squeamish to let the ladies hear confessions? What he think a woman going to hear in that confession box she ain't already heard out on Decatur Street or in her own bed? Sweet darling, the ladies I know, if they ain't done it, they watched it being done.

A pause.

The worst thing I ever done . . . It wasn't selling my body in sex, and it wasn't selling my soul for the pipe and the needle. It was to do with my little girl. Shandra Rose. Shandra Rose with her light eyes, green like fireflies in the dark. First time I saw Shandra Rose's eyes, it struck me her father might've been this john I had that was a cat and dog doctor out by New Orleans East. If he was the one, then Shandra Rose had her some good blood on her daddy side. It was me gave her the bad blood. I don't mean my wildness and my dark ways. I mean my actual blood. I didn't know I was sick till Shandra Rose was born, and the minute she was born, she start dying. The doctor said from the first she wouldn't have much time, and what time she did would be hard time.

A pause.

She passed on a year ago, when she was almost three. It was Mardi Gras week, and I had made her a clown suit out of scraps from a patchwork quilt, because you know how it's always too cold for the littlest ones when Mardi Gras land in February? But this particular Mardi Gras week was a freak of nature. Warm as honey on toast. I fed Shandra Rose her breakfast, oatmeal with raisins and sweet milk, and then I put her in her clown suit and carried her out here on the porch to watch the Indians and the Morguses and such pass by. But soon as I get her out in the sunshine, she start shaking and then she fell out on my neck. I run with her back inside and she's crying about, "Mama, I'm cold. I'm so cold, Mama." So I get up in the bed with her and she's still keep on about, "Mama, I'm cold." I don't know which one of us was shaking the worst. Then she quit shaking. I didn't. I been shaking ever since.

The doctor hollered at me I should've put her in the Children Hospital to die. When she died, I couldn't think what to do from one minute to the next. My girl-friends tried to tell me what to do, but I couldn't hear nothing they said. Something kept on hollering inside my head. Curtis, he finally step forward and arrange for her funeral.

She coughs, then stands and begins to walk to and fro.

One time I read this story in *The Times-Picayune*? About a white woman up in Talisheek watched her child get killed by a drunk man driving a truck down a country road at seven o'clock in the morning. This woman had sent her child out to stand across the road from her house and wait for the schoolbus to pass for her. But when that baby see the truck coming at her, flying down the road like the angel of death, she panic and run right in front of the thing, trying to get back to her mama, who was watching out her kitchen window . . . *Times-Picayune* ran a picture of the mother walking to the graveyard. Pretty-looking blond woman, walking with her head up, and got a white lace bow pinned in her hair. I remembered about that white lace bow the morn-ing of Shandra Rose's funeral. I couldn't find no lace in the house so I made me a headpiece with some feathers I had tore off a dress and some roses I cut out a magazine, and I wore it to the church at the Mass of the Angels. The priest vestments was all in white silk brocade . . . I still got the headpiece around here someplace.

She returns to sit on the glider. She looks out at the street.

Street lamp still burnt out . . . Well, look like Curtis ain't going to make it. I hope him and his plate of beans haven't end up at the police station. It don't matter, I ain't that hungry. Maybe I'll just stay out here a while longer . . . I know I got to quit worrying my mind . . . But see, the worst thing . . . the worst thing is, my little girl came to her mama believing I would save her. But her mama never saved her. Her mama was the very thing had run her down. And I don't ask forgiveness for myself, or mercy, when I go on the way I sometimes do. It's just that some nights, I need . . . I need to kneel in the dark and call the worst thing by its name. By my name. Angèle. Means "angel." Death Angel. Sweet angel mama.

During the preceeding speech, the lights have slowly gone down, until, at the end, Angèle sits in silence, in near-darkness, the red-glassed votive candles flickering, then light fades to black.